THE ESSENTIAL GUIDE TO

Treating Child and Adolescent Anxiety

Over **75** Integrative Strategies to Empower Anxious Kids *and* Their Parents

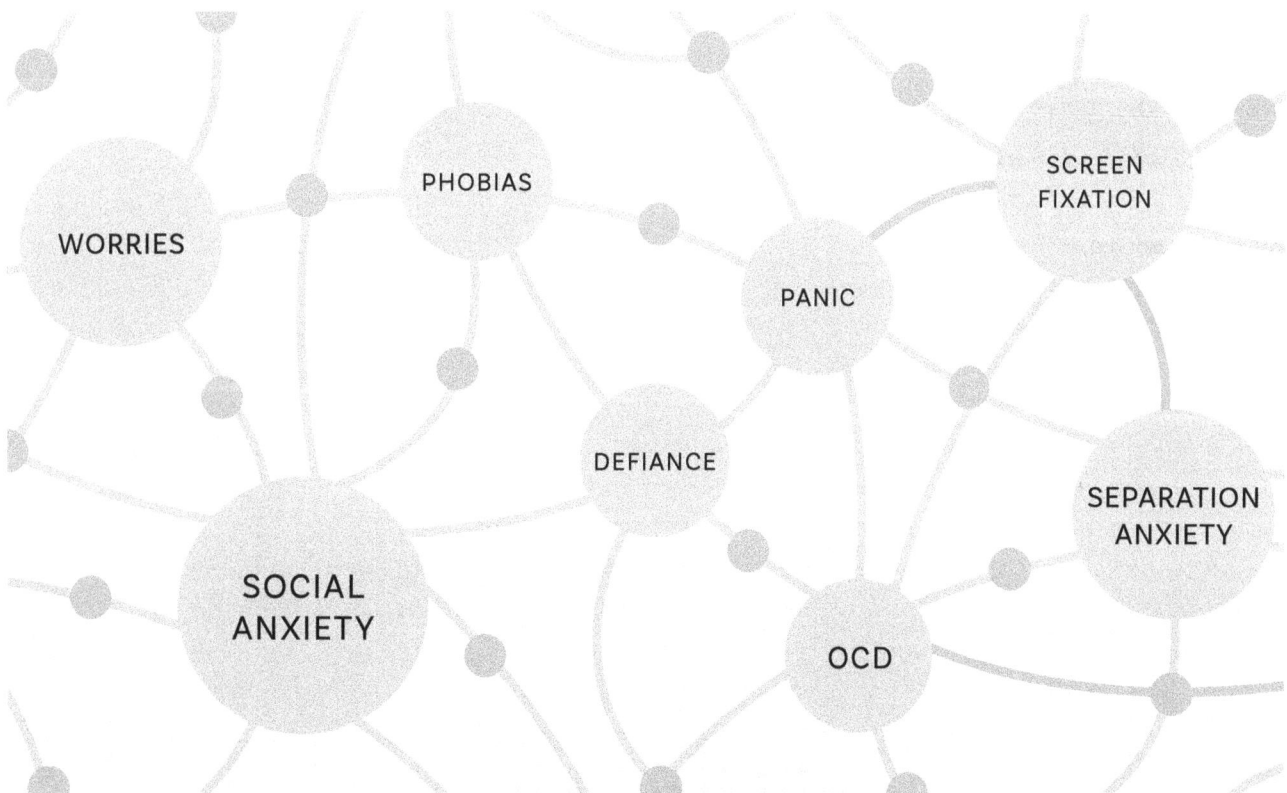

STEVE O'BRIEN, PsyD

The Essential Guide to Treating Child and Adolescent Anxiety
Copyright © 2023 by Steve O'Brien

Published by
PESI Publishing, Inc.
3839 White Ave
Eau Claire, WI 54703

Cover and interior design by Emily Dyer
Editing by Chelsea Thompson

ISBN 9781683736721 (print)
ISBN 9781683736745 (ePDF)
ISBN 9781683736738 (ePUB)

PESI Publishing
pesipublishing.com

Table of Contents

Introduction

The Critical Role of Support

I can still remember how I felt in the early days of my private practice: anxious! Would parents actually show up with their kids and pay for my professional services? Would I be seen as competent, especially since I had yet to reach my thirtieth birthday? Would it be an obstacle that I didn't have kids of my own? Impostor syndrome was starting to set in.

My challenges with anxiety made knocking on doors, handing out cards to family attorneys and pediatricians, and giving free presentations to schools a slow and at times disheartening process. Still, the positive results I was seeing gradually reduced my anxiety, as did the support I received from many kind and credible professionals. Some of the most useful input came from Dr. Ruth Peters, a highly respected child psychologist I met in my first few months of practice who became a trusted mentor. Her invaluable guidance went a long way in helping me find my feet as a beginning clinician and taught me the critical role support plays when faced with anxiety.

Support is perhaps even more vital to children given their developing sense of self. I remember times in my own childhood when I was thankful to receive support from trusted adults, like my fifth-grade teacher who sensed I was struggling emotionally and provided words of kindness and hope. However, there were other times when support was greatly needed but in short supply, leaving me feeling worried, alone, and perhaps worst of all, misunderstood. Remembering the confusion and fear I felt back then reminds me of how the kids entering my office today often feel in their daily lives.

Anxiety disorders are among the most common mental health conditions in children, affecting over 5 million kids in the United States (Lebrun-Harris et al., 2022). Although early identification is improving, anxiety still tends to be underdiagnosed in children, and sadly, most children suffering from anxiety never receive treatment. Plus, contrary to popular opinion, kids do not simply outgrow anxiety disorders. In fact, the presence of childhood anxiety increases the risk of psychological disorders in adulthood. We also know that children reared by highly anxious parents tend to struggle more with the challenges of emerging adulthood (Hiller et al., 2016). Accordingly, our treatment approaches must truly support both children and their caretakers by exchanging anxiety-strengthening dynamics for empowering ones through the use of therapeutic strategies that promote resilience.

Supporting Anxious Kids Means Empowering Anxious Parents

Childhood is not always a carefree time of life, especially given the ever-increasing societal stressors and demands placed on kids. While no one wants to imagine a childhood dominated by worry, fear, and panic, this is the reality for many of today's children.

It goes without saying that a child's challenges with anxiety affect not only the child, but the entire family. Well-intentioned parents, in their efforts to help their children feel safe, may inadvertently enable their child's avoidance of experiences that constitute a healthy, fulfilling childhood. Furthermore, this strong emphasis on safety often limits their child's joy of new adventures and discoveries and ultimately strengthens the anxiety that parents wish to quell.

By the time they enter my office, parents have experienced a multitude of emotions—fear, frustration, irritation, anger. Many have faced judgment and criticism from other parents, extended family, and even some uninformed professionals who see them as responsible for their child's anxiety. Such experiences fuel parents' sense of failure and hopelessness and contribute to a surplus of tension and conflict in the home. After close to 30 years of clinical practice with children and families, I have found that supporting the needs of both anxious children and their parents is vital for promoting lasting change.

People sometimes ask me if working with distressed kids is depressing. My answer: not at all! I truly love my work as a child-family psychologist and consider it a privilege to help families heal together. Moreover, I am often impressed by the resilience of kids and families. Resilience is no easy feat in the face of pervasive social technologies, increasing academic pressures, unpredictable pandemics, and 24-hour news cycles dominated by recurring tragedies.

As the landscape of these stressors continues to grow and shift, I'm continually learning new ways to improve my clinical work. But throughout the unique situations and diverse families I've encountered, one lesson has remained constant: how much kids and parents need practical, nonjudgmental guidance that takes into account child development, family systems, and evidence-based treatments for anxiety. This book reflects the integrative approach I have developed over nearly three decades of therapeutic practice. Whether you are new to the field of child-family mental health or a seasoned clinician, I hope this book supports you in caring for anxious children and their families.

Overview of This Book

With this book, I aim to supplement your therapeutic treatment of anxious children and their parents. I begin, in chapter 1, by providing guidance for setting the stage for treatment and collecting historical data while building rapport with both children and parents. Chapters 2 through 14 focus on integrative, child-friendly methods for treating common DSM-5 anxiety disorders, including individual (child), parent-focused, and family therapy interventions. Chapter 15 addresses school-related anxiety, including strategies for managing anxiety in the classroom as well as homework-related challenges. Chapter 16 covers adjustment-related anxiety in the context of stressors such as divorce, loss, and peer harassment. Finally, chapter 17 offers simple tools for measuring treatment progress and determining the need for additional services, as well as recommendations for preventing childhood anxiety from escalating to a clinical level.

Each chapter ends with a summary of major therapeutic points in the form of "Treatment Highlights." I've also included "Tips With Teens" for additional suggestions when working with adolescents and several "Creative Corners" for stimulating your therapeutic imagination. Numerous handouts and worksheets, designed for both kids and parents, are provided throughout for use in the therapy session or at home to encourage self-reflection, enhance anxiety psychoeducation, promote wellness, and reinforce effective communication and anxiety-management skills.

Writing this book helped me better articulate the process of providing treatment to anxious kids and their parents. I hope that it provides you with greater clarity in the often ambiguous world of child-family therapy and that it stimulates your creativity and confidence for empowering distressed children and their parents in your own unique way.

CHAPTER 1

Setting the Stage: Essentials of Therapy With Anxious Children and Their Parents

The many facets of child anxiety present significant challenges for the therapist beginning treatment with a new family. Exactly who should attend the first session? Should the parents be interviewed with or without the child? What if the parents are in conflict with each other? How do you proceed with an anxious child who is withdrawn or resistant and won't talk with you?

To answer these questions, it helps to bear in mind the three major objectives of an initial session:

- Building rapport

- Collecting information

- Educating about the treatment process

In particular, cultivating effective therapeutic rapport is crucial for helping anxious children and families. Children may be particularly apprehensive and parents highly self-conscious in a new environment with a stranger, even one who intends to help them—after all, getting help requires making themselves vulnerable.

Developing rapport begins from the moment a parent or child sees you. As you form initial impressions of your clients, they are doing the same thing with you. The tone and volume of your voice, as well as your gestures, facial expressions, language, and so forth, will either facilitate or hinder the rapport-building process. Acknowledging and validating their concerns goes a long way in building trust with both anxious kids and their parents.

Who Should Attend the First Session?

Child therapists vary regarding whom they meet with for the initial session. While there is certainly value in a variety of approaches, I believe that meeting with only the parents is the most practical way to begin. An initial parent session provides them the opportunity to be fully candid without the child present.

TIPS WITH TEENS

I make exceptions to this rule with certain adolescents. When a parent first calls my office with concerns about their teen, a few questions are in order. Did the teen request therapy? Is the teen approaching 18 years of age (i.e., 16 years or over)? Does the teen have a preference for attending their first session alone or with their parents—or would the teen prefer that just the parents attend the first session? I've found that some teens feel more comfortable in their initial session when they know their parents have already provided me with some relevant background.

Rapport-Building With Parents: Calibrate Your Approach

Many parents have personalized their child's difficulties and thus believe they have failed as parents. Guilt, shame, and hopelessness can be intense, and parents tend to cope with such feelings by presenting as either fragile, distressed, and hopeless or angry, resentful, and defensive.

To establish a constructive rapport with parents, it's essential to calibrate your therapeutic approach with the parents' disposition. Start by observing each parent's interpersonal style and social comfort level, then modify your relational style accordingly.

- Parents who present as reserved and uncertain need a friendly, informal outline of the session:

  > "Nice to meet you! In a minute, I'll give you the floor to discuss the concerns about your child that brought you in today. Start wherever you like, and I'll ask you questions along the way. Then I'll answer any of your questions about how I work with kids and parents, including how we can most effectively work together."

- Emotionally fragile parents may display excessive self-criticism or overestimate the influence of their parenting on their child. Their tendency to take excessive responsibility for their child's difficulties may make them unaware of other factors shaping their child, such as genetics, peer relationships, or social media. You may need to use a great deal of reflection and validation to support these parents, which can place time constraints on obtaining relevant background information. Commending these parents for seeking professional help by reframing their feelings of failure as love and concern for their child can decrease their distress. Additionally, commenting on the multitude of societal, generational, and peer influences on children can help them recognize that not all of the responsibility lies with them. I recommend speaking one step removed—that is, referring to people in general rather than these parents specifically:

  > "Sometimes parents feel like they've failed their child when in actuality, they love their kids and simply don't know how to help them. Plus, some kids are just more complex or challenging than others."

Children whose parents perceive themselves as failures tend to adopt a similar mindset about themselves. This can lead the child to present as either emotionally fragile or irritable and guarded. The child may then project or displace these feelings onto you as a clinician. Remember that family dynamics greatly affect how children present socially, emotionally, and behaviorally in your treatment setting.

- Some parents present as defensive and accusatory. Parents who have adopted a defensive posture often place blame on others (including each other) for their child's challenges. They are more likely to underestimate their own influence on their child and inflate the influence of other factors, such as school, peers, or the media. When working with such parents, you may find yourself walking a line between providing validation and defusing conflict to obtain an accurate history. A one-step-removed statement can help lower the parents' defenses against each other and you:

  "When concerned parents become frustrated, they sometimes accuse each other of being the core of the problem. But in reality, both parents are doing some things that help and some things that don't. Rather than argue or debate, let's focus on your common goal of helping your anxious child."

- It's not uncommon to find parents leaning in opposite emotional directions. For example, an agitated parent might claim, "This kid just has no respect and my wife babies him," to which the other responds, "You are way too hard on him." In this instance, your goal will be to help the parents depersonalize their child's behavior so that neither accuses the other of causing it. In your first session, explore how these parents came to their beliefs and assess the past experiences that have led to their divergent perspectives and their resentment of each other. Rather than speaking directly to the conflict between them, I once again use a one-step-removed approach:

  "It's common for parents with a challenging child to find fault with each other's parenting style. However, this child brings a lot to the table, regardless of your parenting style. Over time, we can work together to determine what your child needs from each of your different approaches."

- I also look for cues about the fit between each parent and the child (Thomas & Chess, 1977). That is, how easy or challenging does each parent find relating to the child in question versus other children in the family? Knowing how common this is (and how parents often feel guilty about it), I endeavor to normalize it:

  "It's totally natural for parents to 'click' with one child or find them easier to like than another—it doesn't mean they love one child more than the other."

Collecting Information

Most parents need to tell their story—that is, not only express their current concerns about their child but also recount the history that led to this moment. As therapists, we should strive to create a comfortable and conversational climate for parents' frustration, confusion, and fear to be heard and understood.

However, while some parents are at a loss for words, others seem to have an abundance! They may feel pressure to tell you everything, from long-term problems that were minimized or denied to repeated attempts to address issues without success, out of worry that if they forget something, you'll be less equipped to help.

- With these parents, I look for the earliest opportunity to tactfully set limits and add some structure:

  "You're sharing great information that's really helpful. As you know, our time is limited, and I want to be sure that I cover all the essential areas, so excuse me for interrupting at times. When I do, please know that you've given me enough info in that area for now, but I need to ask additional questions so that I'm well prepared for your child's first session. Rest assured that we can schedule other sessions whenever you need to share more information with me."

- Transitional statements are also useful for allowing progression from one topic to another:

  "You've given me a good picture of Tommy's home behavior; now tell me about his behavior at school."

- When I'm working with two parents and one of them is extremely verbal, the other is often very quiet. While it's tempting to continue dialoguing with the more verbal parent, doing so risks alienating the other parent or enabling imbalanced parental dynamics to continue. It also means missing out on a potentially useful perspective. Instead, I gently invite the less verbal parent to comment by stating how each parent's view of their child is vital:

  "Mr. Lopez, what's your take on Tommy's fears?"

Determining a Parent's Developmental Knowledge Base

"He's seven years old and he still doesn't keep his room clean."

"My nine-year-old is still afraid of the dark, no matter how much I reassure her."

Parents differ dramatically in their knowledge of normative child development. Some parents have done a good amount of reading or have learned from experience about developmental processes.

Others have very minimal awareness and perhaps even misguided ideas and expectations about how children become adults.

When parents describe their struggles with their children, I listen carefully and take mental notes so I can look for ways to infuse developmental knowledge into parent sessions over time. For example, if a father expresses frustration with his five-year-old son's inability to follow directions, I look for additional signs of developmentally unrealistic expectations. Next, I mentally prepare to engage both parents in a discussion about the challenges of rearing five-year-olds given their limited ability to cooperate with adult directives. Depending on factors such as the time left in the session and each parent's emotional state and level of receptivity, I may either touch upon the subject in that situation or take note to address the topic in an upcoming parent session.

Obtaining family history of mental health and substance use issues is often an appropriate time in the session to assist parents in grasping the significant influence of genetic factors on their child's development. Discovering parents' knowledge gaps in this area can pave the way for later discussions on topics such as temperament and attachment.

Parents often compare and contrast their own childhood experiences with those of their child without adequate understanding of how factors such as social technology have shaped today's youth. I encourage you to do some reading on Generations Z and Alpha to enhance both your effectiveness with child clients and your ability to educate parents about the unique qualities associated with these generations. (If you're looking for a good place to start, see the Recommended Readings section at the end of this book.)

What to Do When Parents Are in Conflict

It's no surprise that parents of anxious children are often in conflict with each other. This can be due to highly discrepant parenting beliefs or styles but may also be due to unresolved emotional or relationship issues. In some cases, deep-seated resentment on the part of one or both parents serves as a major treatment obstacle. Such resentment is especially prevalent when the parents have recently separated or divorced.

Demonstrating a sense of comfort with their discomfort is critical for regulating the tension. Doing so shows these parents that you are equipped to manage their discord.

- When I sense animosity, I quickly point it out in a nonjudgmental manner:

  "I'm sensing that the two of you have some unresolved issues with each other, which is not uncommon. However, it's positive that you are both here today—it shows that regardless of the tension between you, both of you care about your child's well-being."

- I then encourage the parents to speak more to me than to each other in the initial parent session. I also immediately interrupt heated exchanges with statements such as:

  "I understand that you each have very different beliefs about what is going on with Aaliyah. I can offer each of you separate parent meetings in the near future to share more about these differences, but today you'll help prepare me for working with Aaliyah if we focus on your individual concerns about her."

Educating About Treatment and Wrapping Up the Initial Parent Interview

Often, as I move from collecting information to educating parents about how treatment will progress, a parent will proclaim, "Oh! I forgot to tell you that our dog died suddenly a few months ago." As cognitive psychologists can attest, when we shift topics, it can prompt the recollection of other forgotten information. For that reason, as the session draws to a close, I leave time for parents to share anything I didn't ask about that they think is important for me to know.

Once all information has been shared, I commend each parent for beginning the treatment process and highlight any parental strengths I've observed:

  "Seeking professional counseling for Aaliyah was very timely on your part. I can see how much you feel for her and want her to be less anxious."

Providing education about how I conduct treatment with children and parents includes providing parents with options for giving me information as treatment progresses. I have never been a fan of splitting sessions between a parent and a child, nor of having a parent come in at the beginning or end of a child's therapeutic time. Rather, I invite parents to share information via voicemail or email and encourage them to schedule a parent meeting whenever they have substantial questions or concerns
to discuss.

Typically, I will see a child for three individual sessions before conducting another parent session. In my experience, three sessions are usually adequate to acclimate anxious children to the therapy process and make them comfortable enough to express themselves. Furthermore, the impressions I share in the next parent meeting are likely to be seen as more credible since I am basing them on more than one encounter with the child.

Follow-Up Sessions With Parents

After the initial parent session and three child sessions, I meet with the parents again to obtain their current perception of treatment progress. Essentially, this parent session will enable you to develop a treatment plan. This plan should be developed in collaboration with the parents in a manner that meets the needs of both the child and their parents.

Here is the format I typically use in the second parent meeting:

- First, I invite the parents to update me as to their child's status: "Please update me with any new information about Kyle. Tell me anything that is better, the same, worse, or different since the first time we spoke." Such a request conveys that I do not have skewed expectations about the child in any direction. Rather, I recognize that there are many possibilities in terms of the child's current psychological status. I also ask if they have any additional concerns since our initial meeting.

- While obtaining information about the child's progress is important, it's equally important to determine each parent's current psychological state in this follow-up meeting. Are they pleased with the child's progress thus far? Or are they frustrated, irritated, disappointed, or even disheartened? This knowledge should also inform how you proceed. For example, upon learning that a parent is discouraged, you may discover and explore unrealistic expectations they have for themselves, their child, or both. Conversely, you may encounter parents who only report positive information because they are protecting your feelings as a professional who is trying to help. I find that the more I demonstrate acceptance of all types of current situations with the child, the more candid parents can be with me about their feelings and impressions.

- Depending on the child's level of functioning, I will recommend individual therapy sessions for the child at a frequency from weekly to monthly. I then discuss options for parent meetings, which can also vary in frequency. For example, I may suggest two or three biweekly parent meetings to address topics such as communication and anxiety management. Alternatively, I might simply empower the parents to schedule meetings based on their own needs.

Parent Management: Maintaining Control Without Being Controlling

Were you fortunate enough to receive instruction on how to work with parents in child/adolescent therapy during your graduate training? I'm not referring to behavior modification or communication training, but actual information about how (and how *not*) to manage the parental component of child therapy—for example, how you should respond to a parent's request to speak with you before or after a child's session, or how phone calls or emails from parents should be managed. I was lucky enough to receive a little training in this regard, but I certainly needed a lot more. Instead, I learned the hard way what kinds of approaches to use and avoid with parents.

Later in my career, I served as an associate professor in a clinical psychology doctoral program. Nearly every semester, I witnessed my graduate students' struggles to work effectively with parents during the child/adolescent therapy process. My students' challenges led me to develop my own hard-won insights into a course in parent consultation.

To this day, though, little else has been written on the topic—odd, considering that one of the main requirements in working with children is developing skills in parent management. Many of you have likely heard or even expressed the lament, "I like working with kids, but parents are too frustrating." Too many child therapists lack a system for conducting therapeutic parental consultation.

As mentioned earlier, parents of anxious children can be particularly challenging because they are often anxious themselves. Their anxiety often manifests as a high need for control. These parents will often attempt to direct the therapy with admonitions like "Make sure to talk to him about his problems with worry at bedtime" or "Her anxiety is causing her to fall behind with schoolwork, so we have to figure out a way for her to catch up as soon as possible." I've often had anxious parents insert themselves into a session, insisting that it's necessary for them to speak with their child immediately. Perhaps most commonly, anxious parents tend to want to speak with their child's therapist at the beginning or end of a session. They also may want immediate feedback and advice very early in their child's treatment.

Let's be clear about one thing: Surrendering full control to parents is *not* the way to go. Still, parents do need some input into the therapeutic process. Involving the parents assures them that you adequately grasp their ever-changing concerns about the child and the family. This assurance helps reduce the parents' anxiety, which certainly benefits the child.

How can you maintain adequate control of a child's treatment while meeting the needs of anxious parents? The answer lies in *collaborative control,* a structured yet flexible communication system that keeps parents actively involved and empowered in their child's therapy but does not give them primary control over the child's treatment. This means that when a parent believes therapy should head in a certain direction, such as more focus on combating a phobia, you must balance the parent's request with what is realistically in the child's therapeutic best interest at any given time.

I encourage you to discuss these areas with parents toward the end of the initial session so they know how you will involve them in their child's treatment. Also, be prepared to tactfully restate these procedures, as distressed parents will tend to violate them unintentionally (usually). Setting a friendly but firm precedent is vital for your parent-management system to be effective. It helps the treatment proceed much more smoothly and with less frustration for everyone.

Here is how I recommend approaching this discussion with parents:

- First, share with the parents how and when they can initiate contact with you, as well as how *not* to do so. When parents understand how they can communicate with you, they are much less likely to make sporadic requests (or demands) to speak with you or insert themselves into their child's session. Provide options for how they may relay information and updates about their child. Consider a one-way email setup, in which parents can send you information via email but understand that they will not receive responses from you. Discuss the way you will provide feedback about the session and responses to emails and phone calls. I strongly recommend being as structured and specific as possible—for example: "I return phone calls within 48 hours and can speak by phone for approximately 10 minutes, usually on Tuesdays and Thursdays. If more time is needed, I will ask that we schedule a parent session."

• Inform the parents as to when they will first receive feedback regarding their child's treatment. In my practice, except for crisis situations, the first feedback session occurs after I have seen the child for three visits. This allows me to obtain adequate information at an appropriate pace to provide credible impressions or recommendations.

• Explain that during treatment you will also initiate parent consults whenever you need more information from them or when you have timely recommendations, and invite them to also initiate parent sessions based on their own needs. I find this preferable to parents requesting time at the beginning or end of a child's session, which can interfere with rapport.

• Finally, make it clear that the parents may not insist on family sessions with their child. Decisions about whether and when to meet as a family group will be made between the child and the therapist, although parents may always request a parent session.

TIPS WITH TEENS

• Recognize, validate, and accept resistance rather than attempting to persuade or convince your teen clients. Be highly transparent about your work, especially about how you work with parents. Be willing to share your impressions of their parents in an objective manner.

• Invite discussion about the adults in their lives. Whom do they find annoying? Whom do they relate well with?

How I See Myself as a Parent

Complete the following sentences to gain insight about your role as a parent.

1. I would define or describe parenting as _____

   _____

   _____

2. As a parent, I believe that my top priority is _____

   _____

   _____

3. When it comes to my child, I am responsible for _____

   _____

   _____

4. My greatest parental strength is _____

   _____

   _____

5. An area of parenting for me to work on is _____

   _____

   _____

6. I feel ineffective or negative about my parenting when _____

   _____

   _____

7. Compared with other parents, I am probably _____

_____

_____

8. As a parent, it's hard to admit that _____

_____

_____

9. I expected parenting _____

_____

_____

10. I never expected parenting _____

_____

_____

11. My attitude or beliefs about parenting include _____

_____

_____

12. As a parent, I feel out of control when _____

_____

_____

13. My greatest regret as a parent is _____

_____

_____

14. My greatest reward as a parent is _____

_____

_____

Guidelines for the Initial Session With Children

Unlike adults, children do not typically self-refer for therapy. The decision to begin treatment likely originated from a parent, teacher, or other concerned adult in the child's life. This important distinction from adult therapy requires child therapists to be adept at presenting themselves in a way that allows the child to set the pace of rapport-building.

Instead of a standard greeting, such as "Hi! I'm Dr. O'Brien. It's really nice to meet you," I first greet the parent while simultaneously observing the child's reaction to my presence and letting the child observe me. I then greet the child with a short comment such as "Hi Jeremy! Come on back to my office with Mom." The more opportunity you provide the child to observe you and your therapeutic setting while in the presence of their parent, the more you help the child adjust to the unfamiliar surroundings and allow rapport to develop gradually.

The next hurdle is determining whether and when to ask the parent to leave the room. While this is a matter of clinical judgment, the following protocol can provide some guidance. After explaining the nature of therapy to the child (which I describe in detail in the next section) and introducing them to the therapeutic materials in my office, I then request that the parent wait in the other room: "So, now Emily and I will spend some time together and we will see you in the waiting room when we are finished." If I anticipate that the parent will overly reassure the child, I'll add, "I think Emily will do just fine, and if we need you, we'll come get you." This is important because excessive reassurance from the parent can actually heighten a child's anxiety about separation.

> If separation anxiety is a presenting issue, I prepare parents in their initial session with a plan in case the child should be unable to tolerate their departure from the child's first session. Specifically, I suggest that one parent remain in my office but engaged in another activity, such as reading or completing a questionnaire. Rather than attempting to persuade the child to interact with me, I instead invite them to explore the office while pointing out all the materials at their disposal. Once the child is actively engaged in some kind of activity, I then ask the parent to leave the office in a manner transparent to the child. If this is unsuccessful, the parent can remain in the office until separation can occur, which sometimes takes an additional session.

Preparing Anxious Children for the Initial Therapy Session

For anxious children, the very act of beginning treatment can be highly distressing. Like adults, children worry about whether they will feel comfortable talking to a stranger. Unlike adults, they often have no point of reference as to how a therapy session works or what will happen. Such uncertainty leads to considerable worry before they ever set foot in the office.

Rather than spending a lot of time and energy trying to reassure anxious kids that therapy is a "safe space" and that I'm "here to help," I've learned that it's more effective to begin familiarizing children with the details of therapy before I even lay eyes on them. Toward the end of my initial session with the parents, I describe a step-by-step format for giving their child a visual-sequential explanation of what will happen during the initial therapy session.

I suggest that the parents begin by describing my waiting room and office in simple terms that the child can visualize, followed by a description of the sequence of events that will occur:

> "When we walk into the building, we'll say hi to Miss Paula, who will be at her desk behind a little window, and then we'll sit in some green chairs. In a few minutes, Dr. O'Brien will walk in and say hello. Then you and I will follow him to his office, and you'll see a soft couch, comfy chairs, and shelves with lots of toys, games, and art materials. Dr. O'Brien will tell us a little bit more about how he works with kids and parents, and when you're comfortable, I'll go back and wait for you in the other room. When you and Dr. O'Brien are done talking and playing, he will walk you back to the waiting room to see me."

This visually descriptive step-by-step explanation often helps put the child at ease, making for a much more productive first session. I provide additional guidelines in chapter 2 for how you can adapt the initial child interview to accommodate children with different temperaments.

Rapport-Building With Children: The "Ease In" Approach

While some professionals believe that child therapy should begin with an array of questions—"Tell me about yourself," "How do you feel about your family?" "Do you like school?"—this method is seldom a good place to start with anxious children. Children are regularly bombarded by questions from their parents and other well-intentioned adults, from what they learned at school that day to whether they brushed their teeth, and short answers like "fine" or "I don't know" are typical in response to this often overwhelming demand for information. This is even more true for anxious children, who already likely have an abundance of racing thoughts and mixed feelings about the various changes in their environment. This is why it's vital for therapists to "ease in" to the rapport-building process.

While there is no definitive method for determining when rapport has been established with the child, visual signs such as a more relaxed posture and increased eye contact are often good indicators that the child is ready for some level of conversation. However, if your initial questions are met with shrugs or "I don't know," then attempts at verbal discourse should be postponed. Instead, invite the child to explore your office. I keep a small basket of fidget items close to the child's reach—playing with these items can help relieve tension while eliciting the child's thoughts, questions, and possible familiarity or past experiences with these items.

Creative Corner

Diving into a child's interests in gaming, media, art, or music builds rapport in a powerful way. Remember, children rarely receive uninterrupted attention from a genuinely invested adult while explaining their interests.

TIPS WITH TEENS

- Normalize initial discomfort with therapy.
- Reduce self-consciousness by commenting on the types of concerns you hear from teens.
- Share information about yourself as a professional working with adolescents.

Respecting Confidentiality While Keeping Parents in the Loop

One of the major challenges in working with children is balancing their confidentiality with parental involvement. I've known a number of child therapists who alienate parents by rigidly guarding patient privacy. In my view, this prevents much-needed parental intervention and only increases the frustration and misunderstanding in the home. Child therapy outcomes are much more effective when parents are informed enough to understand their child and learn new ways of relating and responding to them.

On the other hand, I have heard children express mistrust of confidentiality: "My last therapist told my parents everything I said." Not only does this approach interfere with rapport, but it makes it harder to obtain credible information and strengthens this child's mistrust of adults.

To balance these concerns, I explain to the child how confidentiality is different from keeping secrets from their parents:

> "Confidentiality means that I won't tell other people what you say to me unless I ask you first if it's okay. It's up to you if you want to tell other people what you say in here—you get to decide that—but I will keep what you say private. Now, there may be some things that I have to tell your parents for safety reasons—for example, if I think you might do something that could hurt you, or if I learn about another kid who's being hurt. If something like that comes up, you and I can decide together how to tell your parents. At times, your parents will also meet with me. I will give them some privacy, too, but if I think there is something important for you to know, I will tell you during our next time together."

Collecting Information: Tips for Child-Friendly Interviewing

Once you determine that a child client understands therapy and your role, they appear relatively at ease, and you sense an adequate level of rapport, you can begin collecting information in a child-friendly interview. Clinical knowledge and judgment regarding child development should serve as your guide in selecting questions and comments that elicit relevant information about the child. Lack of such knowledge is likely to cause therapists to either over- or underestimate a child's ability to express thoughts, feelings, and so forth, resulting in minimally useful interchanges. (The Recommended Readings section at the end of this book includes many titles that will help bolster your developmental knowledge base.)

When you determine that a child is able to engage in discussion, it's helpful to give the child two or three options for how to proceed. I present each option gradually and with a one-step-removed approach in speaking.

- I often start with an overview of what I'm about to offer and why:

  "When kids have never been here before, sometimes it's kind of hard to know what to say or do. I usually give them three choices for getting started."

- One option is to talk about something important to the child, such as one of their major frustrations about school or family life:

  "Some kids already have an idea of something they'd like to talk about, such as something they really don't like or something they wish were different."

- A second option involves discussing the child's favorite activities, including online interests:

  "Lots of kids start by talking about things they like to do, either by themselves or with others, that they find fun or interesting."

- A third is a behavioral option, in which I invite the child to explore the play and art materials in my office. This is especially helpful if the child demonstrates a limited tolerance or ability to remain seated.

  "The third choice is to look at and play with anything on the shelves, either by yourself or with me. I also have drawing materials you can use if you'd like."

It's important to note that while options give anxious kids a sense of control, too many options can feel overwhelming. Also, for very young or highly anxious children, I typically omit the first option since it requires a level of self-reflection beyond their capacity, as well as disclosure of potentially sensitive content.

- Rather than asking open-ended questions during the interview, offer the child emotionally balanced options for their answer. Not only will this help reduce the chance of the child feeling overwhelmed, but it will also give you a chance to note whether the child seems to highlight more negatives than positives, or vice versa. Frame the questions in a commentary fashion and keep using the one-step-removed approach:

  > "Some kids decide to talk about things they like, or things they don't like, about school. What would you like to start with?"

- Avoid following one question too quickly with another. Otherwise, the child may feel interrogated, leading them to either tell you what they think you want to hear, give simplistic answers, or simply shut down. Instead, make comments that show you are listening and, ideally, normalize or validate any thoughts and feelings the child shares:

  > "So you really like sports and gaming. It seems like you enjoy a challenge and getting better at what you do."

Take note of their reaction to your questions and comments. Many children will appreciate your attempts to connect and respond with a resounding "Yes, I love it when I get to the next level!" Others may react minimally, with a subtle head nod. Still others may react defensively: "Nah, not really."

- With teens, especially those who appear more mistrusting, I sometimes present a fourth option: to share some information from my initial parent session. I usually start with something that the teen is likely already familiar with:

  > "Your parents shared with me about how much you dislike school."

Afterward, I pause to observe their reaction and give them an opportunity to respond. Depending on how they respond, I might clarify that their parents' perceptions can differ from their own. I also typically follow every couple of parental concerns I share with something positive:

  > "They also mentioned that you have a good sense of humor."

This approach highlights my transparency to the teen and tends to promote trust—they see me as a straightforward therapist who is not de facto on their parents' "side."

With this step, I am careful to avoid highly sensitive information, as well as anything that might be unknown to the teen. Earlier in my career, I made a serious mistake with a teen when I asked him a question about an extended family member's substance use challenge; it turned out he wasn't aware of the issue. Some extra parent and family sessions were then needed to transparently process my significant misstep.

- Finally, inform and empower the child about their treatment options:

> "In here, you have lots of choices. You and I will have our time together, but if you ever want one of your parents or family members to be in a session with you, just let me know."

Remember, the initial interview with an anxious child is a mutual observation. While you are observing the child's numerous developmental and psychosocial factors, the child is observing your gestures, expressions, emotional tone, and so forth, especially in response to their comments and behaviors. Attuned child therapists continually self-regulate to help the anxious child self-regulate (Delahooke, 2017). This helps keep the child's anxiety level within a manageable range so they can gradually show more of themselves at their own pace.

Avoiding Alignments While Advocating for All

One of the many challenges in working with children (especially preteens and adolescents) is maintaining empathy for both the kid and their parents so that you can effectively advocate for all parties. While empathy can be difficult to uphold with a resistant kid or a highly authoritarian parent, these are the cases in which empathy and advocacy are most needed. Respecting the child's resentment about being "forced" into therapy or the parent's anxiety about feeling ineffective is key to developing an advocacy strategy.

Some of the best strategies begin by acknowledging and validating each person's underlying feelings. Statements like "It's not easy being here when it wasn't your choice" or "It's really frustrating when kids won't listen and comply when you're only looking out for their best interest" reflect genuine understanding and may soften resistant preteens and parents. You can then follow up with statements like "Let's see what we can come up with so that you feel better about being here" or "We'll work together so that you feel less frustrated and more effective."

Educating About Treatment: Explaining Therapy to Anxious Kids

I have found that one of the best ways to help anxious children adjust to therapy is to inform them about the nature of therapy in simple, relatable, age-appropriate terms.

- Start by reiterating and expanding on what their parents have told them to prepare for the session:

> "The times when we meet are called 'therapy sessions.' These sessions are for you to talk, play, and draw however you like and with privacy. Medicines and shots are not part of our sessions, but sometimes talking and playing is like medicine because it can help kids feel better."

- Next, describe your role as a therapist and explain the purpose of therapy in a one-step-removed manner:

> "My job as a therapist has three parts. First, I get to know kids very well, like how they think and feel about lots of things. Second, I give them privacy, which we will talk more about. Third, I help them come up with ideas to feel better and less worried. This is a place where kids can say just about anything, and where they can also play, draw, or just explore the office. I also talk with parents to help them with ideas too."

Child-Focused Family Sessions

Family therapy sessions can be an excellent venue for actively advocating on behalf of both children and parents. They are also essential when family dynamics are a significant contributor to the child's anxiety. Still, such sessions should not occur without adequate preparation. Bringing anxious, resistant kids and frustrated, fuming parents into family sessions without plenty of planning can prevent or even regress treatment progress. However, a particular approach I refer to as *child-focused family therapy* allows therapists to advocate for both kids and parents so that family contributors to anxiety can be addressed.

If you feel a family session is therapeutically indicated, begin by preparing the child for this experience during one or more of their individual sessions. Consider the following step-by-step approach for doing so:

- **Explore** the child's feelings about a possible family session. If the child is feeling resistant, apprehensive, or hopeless about the prospect of a session with their parents, work with them to determine what is causing their negative outlook. It may be anything from the child's fear of their parent yelling or lecturing to a feeling of being "ganged up on" by the adults. Some children may not trust their parents to be honest and genuine in session. Some may fear that their parents will be agitated following the session, with repercussions for the child once they return home. If you determine that a child is not adequately comfortable with a family session, I suggest holding off on pursuing a family session until the child is amenable; any family therapy with a resistant child is likely to be an uphill and minimally productive endeavor. Alternatively, you can inform the parents that you believe one or more parent sessions would be more productive.

- **Validate** the child's feelings and ask what, if anything, could make them feel differently about a family session. That is, what would need to happen in a family session that would be a positive, worthwhile outcome for the child?

- **Determine** whether the child's desired outcome could become a reality and if so, to what degree. If not, offer any possible alternative outcome that could be appealing to the child:

> "While it's not possible for your parents to excuse you from chores and homework, it may be possible for you to earn extra privileges for doing those things."

- **Offer** to serve as the child's advocate and communication assistant. I often tell kids that while I can't guarantee that things will go their way, I can work with them to help their parents understand their thoughts and feelings; I can also set limits on parents should they begin to raise their voices, lecture, or similar and jump in whenever I think their parents are making them really uncomfortable. Remind the child that you may also need to set limits on their own communication or speak for them so that their parents respond in a more optimal manner.

- **Prepare** the parents before conducting a child-focused family session. This is especially important when working with highly permissive, authoritarian, anxious, angry, or personality-disordered parents. Follow the same steps used in preparing the child, and be sure to inform the parents that you may interrupt them during the session, speak for them, or ask them to direct their comments to you rather than to their child. Explain that you will only do these things when you discern that it will help the session go smoothly and be more productive. Moreover, such actions convey respect for the child's limits and model effective communication for the parents.

- **Begin and end** the family therapy session with just the child. Beginning with the child alone allows the two of you to review and confirm what the child wants to address with their parents during the family session. This time also allows the two of you to develop an agreed-upon phrase or gesture that can signal the child's need for the parents to leave the room, should the child begin to feel highly uncomfortable. Then you and the child can process the interactions afterward. Doing this helps to maintain the child's sense of control in the treatment.

TIPS WITH TEENS

- Assess the quality of the teen-parent relationship carefully before considering a family therapy session.

- Anxious teens often have difficulty trusting adults, especially if they feel betrayed, so approach family therapy sessions with caution.

- Explore and process the teen's worries and concerns about a possible family session. Develop mutually agreed-upon signals for excusing parents from the family session. Serve as the teen's voice and advocate while validating the parents' concerns.

- Consider follow-up parent sessions to process challenging family sessions.

Rethinking Expectations, Goals, and Progress

American psychologist and professor Barry Schwartz (2005) has said that "the secret to happiness is low expectations." While some may feel otherwise, most therapists would likely agree that managing expectations is a useful skill, especially for anxious kids, parents, and of course therapists.

In this field, it's not uncommon to encounter parents who expect their anxious kids to eventually be anxiety-free. Kids themselves often harbor the same hope. If only we therapists were that skilled! Instilling realistic expectations in the kids and families we serve is an important early step in the treatment process. Rather than looking to the therapist as the "problem fixer," children and parents should view us as professionals who can assist and empower them in addressing problems in a practical manner with a reasonable assurance of a positive outcome.

I encourage parents to view their role in a similar fashion. Rather than any one person taking on the responsibility of "fixing" their child's issues, the child, parents, and therapist work together to reduce the intensity, frequency, duration, and impact of anxiety through better identification and management. This often includes the therapist assisting the parents in determining which desired treatment outcomes are realistic given the child's current level of functioning. For example, when working with a parent who insists that their child should stop worrying about contracting an illness, the therapist can reframe the goal to the child learning to manage worry more effectively. To take an analogy from baseball, we may not hit home runs one after another, but with plenty of practice, well-managed losses, and enough base hits, we can come out ahead when the season ends. Rather than aiming for a total change of personality, we set our sights on developing healthier mindsets through education, awareness, and skill-building, with an ongoing goal of improved quality of life for kids and their families.

Learning About Expectations

Our expectations can have a lot to do with how much and what kinds of anxiety we experience. Finish the sentences below to learn about the role your expectations may play in your anxious thoughts and feelings.

1. When it comes to school, I expect _____

   _____

   _____

2. I expect my parents to _____

   _____

   _____

3. What I expect most from myself is _____

   _____

   _____

4. I expect my friends to _____

   _____

   _____

5. My parents expect me to _____

   _____

   _____

6. My friends expect me to _____

   _____

   _____

7. I expect my teachers to _____

_____

_____

8. Most adults expect kids to _____

_____

_____

9. My teachers expect me to _____

_____

_____

10. I expect my life or my future _____

_____

_____

Identifying and Managing My Expectations

Parents' expectations of themselves and others can be a major contributor to anxiety. Complete the sentences below to help you consider how modifying certain expectations can help ease your child's anxiety and your own.

1. As a parent, I expect my child to _____

   _____

   _____

2. I expect a mother to _____

   _____

   _____

3. I expect a father to _____

   _____

   _____

4. As a parent, I expect myself to _____

   _____

   _____

5. I expect my child's teachers to _____

   _____

   _____

6. I expect my family to be _____

   _____

   _____

7. I expect extended family members to _____

_____

_____

8. I expect those caring for my child to _____

_____

_____

9. I expect my child's other parent to _____

_____

_____

10. I expect my child's therapist/counselor to _____

_____

_____

TREATMENT HIGHLIGHTS

Initial Interview With the Parents

- Observe each parent's interpersonal style and social comfort level, then modify your relational style accordingly.

- Use transitional statements for tactful interruption and to add structure to an initial parent session.

- Look for ways to infuse developmental knowledge into parent sessions over time. Explore the parents' awareness of genetic, temperamental, and other nonparental factors on child development.

- Check with the parents to see if there is anything you didn't ask that is important to know; highlight any parental strengths; and provide education about how treatment will proceed.

Initial Session With the Child

- Learn about the child's temperament before your initial session and modify your initial greeting and interactions accordingly.

- Describe therapy in age-appropriate, concrete language to help reduce initial anxiety in children. For example: "Sometimes talking, playing, and drawing can make kids feel better."

- Inform the child that therapy also includes you meeting with their parents in separate sessions because "your parents also need time to talk and get new ideas for helping you."

- Explain that confidentiality means privacy but also relay the limits of confidentiality.

- Present low-demand discussion options, such as the child's favorite places and activities.

- Encourage minimally verbal children to explore the materials in your office.

- Keen observation of play is often a critical component.

- Respect and validate the resistant teen's perspective.

CHAPTER 2

Anxiety Psychoeducation: The First Intervention

A critical aspect of our therapeutic work is psychoeducation—that is, providing children and families with useful information that paves the way for other interventions. Anxiety psychoeducation empowers kids and parents with knowledge that can help them feel less hopeless and more confident in their ability to manage anxiety. Understandably, psychoeducation has more impact when your child clients and their parents trust you and see you as a credible source of information. Thus, while such education should occur early in treatment, it must not precede adequate rapport. In addition, psychoeducation should continue over the course of treatment to solidify knowledge and offer more in-depth information as needed.

Teaching Parents About Their Child's Overactive Brain

Parents often struggle to grasp what is going on in their anxious child's brain. Many attempt to use logic to understand and soothe their child: "Why are you anxious? You know that I always come back to pick you up from school at the same time!" But logic is of little use in comprehending a child's overactive brain. That's why it's vital to provide parents with practical information about how their child's brain operates—specifically, how the amygdala (the "protector" part of the brain) hijacks the cerebral cortex (the "manager" part). Such understanding leads to more empathy for the child, which can facilitate a calmer, less frustrated response from parents.

Signs of Anxiety in Kids

Anxiety can show up in all kinds of different ways, including our thoughts, emotions, body sensations, and behaviors. For example, some kids have a lot of worries and negative thoughts, while other kids more often get stomachaches or feel dizzy. Learning how you experience anxiety—in your own unique way—will help you recognize when you're starting to feel anxious so you can take steps to feel better.

Read through the following list of things that many kids think, feel, or do when they're anxious, and mark any that are true for you. If you have other anxiety signals that aren't included, feel free to add them to the list. Then, consider sharing this worksheet with an adult you trust so they'll be better able to support you.

Note to parents: You can also use this list to identify signs of anxiety that you observe in your child.

When I'm Anxious, I Might . . .

Have Thoughts Like These:

☐ Racing thoughts (so many/so fast that it's overwhelming)

☐ Negative thoughts about myself or others

☐ Lots of worries, like thinking something bad could happen

☐ Doubts about myself, like whether I'm smart or look okay

☐ Difficulty focusing or concentrating

☐ Bad dreams or worrying about having them

☐ Thoughts about losing control

☐ Frightening or disturbing images in my mind

Have Feelings Like These:

☐ Feeling very frustrated with myself or others

☐ Feeling irritated or annoyed without knowing why

☐ Feeling angrier than I think I should

☐ Feeling like I'm empty inside

☐ Feeling like things are not okay

☐ Feeling disconnected from others or from myself

☐ Feeling like I'm not real or the world around me isn't real

☐ Feeling numb or emotionless

Feel Like This in My Body:

- ☐ Headache
- ☐ Feeling hot, sweaty, or flushed
- ☐ Uncomfortable skin sensations (e.g., like bugs are crawling on my skin)
- ☐ Heart pounding or tightness in my chest
- ☐ Feeling like it's hard to breathe
- ☐ Feeling like I'm choking or it's hard to swallow
- ☐ Feeling dizzy
- ☐ Voice shaking or difficulty speaking
- ☐ Feeling less or more hungry than usual
- ☐ Stomachache or feeling like I might throw up
- ☐ Using the bathroom a lot, or feeling like I have to go
- ☐ Muscles feeling tense or tight
- ☐ Feeling shaky, jittery, or jumpy
- ☐ Trouble falling asleep or waking up during the night

Do Things Like This:

- ☐ Squirming or fidgeting
- ☐ Shouting or yelling
- ☐ Complaining, arguing, or whining
- ☐ Throwing or breaking things
- ☐ Hitting or fighting with others
- ☐ Crying or tearing up
- ☐ Being hyper or not able to control my movements
- ☐ Asking others the same questions many times
- ☐ Staying near others because I don't want to be alone
- ☐ Checking things over and over, like whether doors are locked or my hands are clean
- ☐ Repeating words or counting things (out loud or in my mind)
- ☐ Arranging or organizing things to be "just right"
- ☐ Following morning or bedtime routines in the "right" order
- ☐ Trying to avoid things I have to do, like homework or going to school
- ☐ Hiding or running away

Understanding Your Child's Overactive Brain

The brain is a very complex organ, and we continue to learn more about how an anxious brain operates. The following is a simplified overview of what is happening in your child's brain when they experience anxiety:

- Anxiety is the result of communication between several brain regions: the **amygdala**, the **stria terminalis**, the **hippocampus**, and the **prefrontal cortex**. These four brain regions are connected by neural pathways and work together to determine whether a situation is threatening. The brain activity in these four areas serves as an "anxiety detective region" that either perpetuates or reduces anxiety.

- The "anxiety detective region" sends signals downstream to the **motor cortex**, **brainstem**, and **neuroendocrine system**, where they are evaluated as possible signs of anxiety. Next, these signals initiate anxiety responses by altering heart and respiration rate and by triggering defensive or avoidant behavior to reduce perceived danger. Excessive, debilitating anxiety (e.g., panic attacks) can happen when the brain's anxiety pathways misinterpret incoming signals as threatening rather than benign.

- Repeated exposure to perceived threats causes the anxiety-producing pathways to become unusually hyperactive and thus more likely to interpret various stimuli as dangerous. When threat is perceived, the amygdala signals the **adrenal gland** to release two chemicals: **adrenaline** and **cortisol**. The overactive brain has a highly reactive amygdala, which means more frequent release of adrenaline and cortisol, causing a flight (avoidance), fight (verbal/physical aggression) or freeze (numbness or dread) response.

- Children differ as to which symptoms of anxiety are most problematic for them. For some, racing, negative thoughts and worries are the main issues. For others, physical symptoms like sweating, chest tightness, or stomach discomfort are most distressing, which can lead to panic. Some children zone out, shut down, or dissociate (appear detached and emotionless), while others exhibit highly ritualized, repetitive, or compulsive behavior.

Taking Children on a Journey Through the Brain

While kids learn about the body in health class, instruction about the brain is often lacking. Understanding the basics about brain function is a necessary first step in treatment for anxiety. I often use age-appropriate visuals (kid-friendly brain illustrations and videos) as I take kids on a journey through their brain. Below are suggestions for how to describe the various brain areas, adapted from a useful book entitled *Mindfulness for Children* (Afzal, 2018), followed by a helpful child worksheet.

Overview

"Your brain is a marvelous organ, and it enables everything you do, think, and feel. Different parts of your brain work together, although some parts tend to help most with certain kinds of things. Sometimes certain brain areas can work too hard or not function as well as they should. But keeping the brain relaxed can really help it perform well."

"The Manager" (The Prefrontal Cortex)

"The prefrontal cortex is like the manager of your brain. It helps you think before you act, make good choices, plan ahead, and get things done, like homework and chores. It also helps you be creative and solve all kinds of problems. Sometimes the manager works really hard for too long, which can tire it out. To do its best work, the manager needs the brain to get enough rest."

"The Librarian" (The Hippocampus)

"The hippocampus is your brain's librarian. It oversees all of your memories, including everything you learn. Since our brains learn so much in our lifetimes, the librarian cannot find every memory, but even when the memory is hard to find, it's still there! If you have a well-rested brain, the manager can help the librarian, and sometimes new learning can also help your librarian find older memories."

"The Kind Friend" (The Insula)

"The insula does many things, including helping you be aware of your body and control your movement. But it's also the part of the brain that helps you feel kindness, both toward others and toward yourself. So, the insula makes it possible for us to experience empathy and compassion. The cool thing is that the more we practice kindness, the nicer we become to both ourselves and other people!"

"The Security Guard" (The Amygdala)

"The amygdala is like your security guard and protector—it detects danger and keeps you safe. But it can also make you worried and scared when there is nothing to fear! Everybody's security guard is a bit different. Some of us have one that detects danger when there really is no danger. For example, all security guards do an excellent job of detecting a fire in the house so we can escape. But some guards think the smell of burnt toast means there's a dangerous fire in the kitchen. To help our protectors not overreact, we need to learn how to relax our brains."

A Journey Through Your Amazing Brain

Your brain can do so many different things! It's almost like your brain has different departments, each with a special and important job. The manager helps you think before you act, the librarian stores everything you learn and experience, the kind friend helps you feel compassion for yourself and others, and the security guard keeps you safe. But sometimes our security guards work way too hard to keep us safe when we actually are safe already.

Use the brain picture to draw or write in the following for each area of the brain:

The Manager
A good choice you've made

The Librarian
Something you've
learned or remember

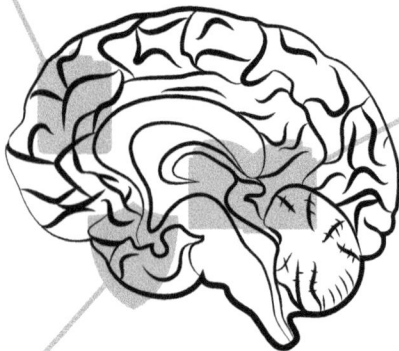

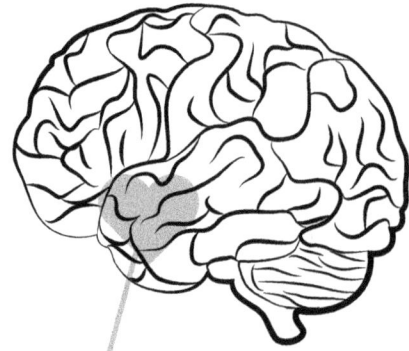

The Security Guard
Something that scares
or worries you

The Kind Friend
An act of kindness

How to Relax Your Brain

Your brain works best when you are relaxed. Many studies have taught us that a few simple things really help the brain be calmer and more peaceful:

1. Slow, deep breathing in through your nose and out through your mouth

2. Long, gentle stretches of your body

3. Rubbing the back of your neck and other tight muscle areas

4. Imagining peaceful scenes, like lying on a beach or swinging in a hammock

5. Calming, positive self-talk, like this: "I can help my brain relax if I concentrate on my breathing and use my peaceful imagination"

6. Listening to relaxing music or other peaceful sounds, like the sound of the ocean

7. Soothing smells like vanilla, lavender, eucalyptus, or sandalwood

Learning How You Can Relax

Just like you prefer certain foods and activities, your brain prefers certain ways to relax. While all of us should practice breathing and stretching, use the questions below to figure out what kinds of things help your unique brain feel peaceful and calm.

1. A place that I find very peaceful and relaxing is _____

   because when I'm there I see _____,

   hear_____, and

   feel _____.

   I also notice that when I'm there, I feel _____

   on my skin and my thoughts are _____.

2. One of my favorite smells in the kitchen is _____.

   A smell I enjoy outside in nature is _____.

3. Two colors that make me feel peaceful are _____ and _____.

4. I feel very relaxed and cozy when I feel these kinds of materials, fabrics, or textures: _____

   _____.

5. The types of music or songs that make me feel calm and happy are _____

   _____.

   Other sounds I find calming are _____

   _____.

Psychoeducation for Parents: Temperament and Goodness of Fit

Parents with more than one child are often perplexed at how different they are from each other. ("We raised them similarly, but they are like night and day!") When they ask me how this is possible, I tell them the simplest answer: Their children's brains are different.

In the late 1970s, psychiatrists Alexander Thomas and Stella Chess conducted seminal research into child temperament that continues to be relevant today. *Temperament* refers to a person's innate personality, manifested by how they react to and interact with their environment. After extensive study of factors such as activity level, distractibility, adaptability, attention span/persistence, and dominant mood quality, Thomas and Chess (1977) found three general temperamental patterns: easy, slow-to-warm-up, and difficult. While temperament can change to some degree over time, it is relatively stable until adolescence or, in many cases, until early adulthood.

- **Easy-tempered infants** tend to have a positive mood, adjust well to new people and environments, and follow predictable, consistent patterns of eating and sleeping. (These are the kinds of infants that you want next to you on a long flight!) When problems develop, finding solutions to soothe or satisfy the child is typically less challenging.

- **Slow-to-warm-up** infants may be initially mellow, but they are prone to colic, express negative moods intensely, and have challenges adjusting to novel people and places. As they age, these children seem most prone to anxiety.

- **Difficult-tempered** infants have very high energy levels, exhibit intense emotional reactions of all kinds, and tend to be quite challenging for caregivers. As they develop, they are more likely to exhibit behavior problems, such as aggression and impulsivity.

Temperament applies to parents as well. Since each parent brings their own personality style to child-rearing, the compatibility or "goodness of fit" between an infant's temperament and the parent's personality will influence the attachment relationship.

Awareness of temperament and goodness of fit is vital for therapists to assist parents in modifying their communication and behavioral responses to their children. In addition, parents who understand these concepts are often less prone to the guilt and self-criticism that comes from taking excessive responsibility for their child's challenges.

For these reasons, temperament-based intervention has become a critical component of evidenced-based treatments for children. Knowing a child's temperament before the first therapeutic encounter can help ensure a better rapport-building process and can guide the pace and timing of interventions in individual therapy. In addition, understanding a child's temperament empowers you to make better clinical decisions in parent consultation and family therapy sessions.

Identifying Your Child's Temperament

Place a check mark next to statements that describe your child most of the time. While many children will have some qualities of other temperaments, the column with the most checks will likely best describe your child's temperament.

Easy Temperament	Slow-to-Warm-Up Temperament	Difficult Temperament
☐ Moderate energy level	☐ Below-average energy level	☐ High energy/hyperactive
☐ Generally positive mood	☐ Often moody, negative, worried, or whiny	☐ Often boisterous or angry
☐ Good attention span and persistence with most tasks	☐ High attention span and persistence on interest	☐ Short attention span; low persistence with mundane tasks
☐ Consistent eating and sleeping patterns	☐ Picky eater and trouble sleeping	☐ Unpredictable or erratic eating and sleeping
☐ Can be distracted but refocuses with assistance	☐ Intense hyperfocus that can become obsessive, or often absent-minded or "zoned out"	☐ Easily distracted and difficult to redirect
☐ Adjusts well to new people, places, and situations	☐ Slow to adjust to new people, places, and situations	☐ Adjustment is largely dependent on mood or motivation
☐ Socially skilled and comfortable	☐ Shy or reserved, especially with new people	☐ Socially comfortable but domineering
☐ Normal startle response	☐ Often fearful, with a strong startle response	☐ Strong and aggressive startle response
☐ Emotionally expressive and reactive to an average level	☐ Difficulty expressing thoughts and feelings	☐ Intense emotional and behavioral reactions
☐ Considerate and empathetic but not overly sensitive	☐ Highly compassionate, sensitive, and empathetic	☐ Caring but somewhat self-centered
☐ Manages stress fairly well; relatively resilient ("bounces back" easily)	☐ Limited stress-management skills, resulting in emotional shutdown or outbursts	☐ Limited stress-management skills expressed as emotional or physical volatility
☐ Will seek help when needed	☐ Frequently asks for help; highly dependent	☐ Fiercely independent
☐ Age-appropriate emotional/behavioral self-control	☐ Minimal emotional self-control	☐ Minimal behavioral and emotional self-control
☐ Enjoys activities both alone and with others	☐ Prefers solitary creative activities	☐ Often seeks novel and high-energy activities with others
☐ Body-related complaints are moderate and credible	☐ Very prone to body-related complaints (e.g., headaches)	☐ Body-related complaints are overlooked or dramatized

Increasing "Goodness of Fit" Between You and Your Child

As the parent of an anxious child, you may be blaming yourself for your child's struggles. This is not accurate and certainly not helpful. Instead, take a thoughtful look at how you and your child relate with each other. How does your child typically respond to you, especially when they are anxious, and how do you respond to your child?

We've explored your child's temperament; now, what about your own? When it comes to parenting (and perhaps other areas of life), do you consider yourself relatively laid-back, or keyed up and worried, or easily agitated and frustrated?

Monitoring your own reactions to your child's distress is an important part of assisting them with managing their anxiety. Remember, we can't expect kids to be well regulated around poorly regulated adults. Your child absolutely senses your emotional state, regardless of their age or how much attention they seem to be paying. When you practice maintaining a reasonable sense of calm assurance without much emotional intensity or excessive reassurance, you cultivate a solid interpersonal climate for your child that helps them better manage their anxiety.

Yes, this is easier said than done. One communication tactic that can help is something I call **say it versus show it.** This technique involves simply labeling unpleasant or uncomfortable feelings such as anger, frustration, or disappointment, rather than expressing them in a heightened or dramatic fashion.

For example, rather than raising your voice and gesturing with your hands when you're feeling frustrated with your child, maintain a calm but firm disposition as you state your feelings:

> "I'm very frustrated with your behavior right now, and I want us to figure out how we can both be calm and get through this."

When you are worried about your child's distress, express faith in their ability to cope with support:

> "I see that you are scared because I'm leaving, but Mrs. Martinez is here to help you, and I know you can do this with her help. I'll see you after school."

Say it versus show it won't always be enough to resolve an anxiety-ridden situation, but it should at least prevent a negative interchange from escalating. While you can't necessarily rid your child of all anxiety, you can take comfort in knowing that you are not contributing to it.

Initial Interview Guidelines by Temperament

I can still remember one of my very early initial interviews with a young child—let's call him Devon. I was an intern in my final year of graduate school working at a community mental health center in Miami. Devon was an extremely active five-year-old boy presenting with aggressive behavior at home and school. As Devon was running around my office, exploring virtually every inch of the room, I was attempting to engage him in what I thought were very relevant questions. "How old are you?" "What grade are you in?" and probably one of the worst questions, "Why do you think you are here today?" Despite his minimal responses and continuous hyperactivity, I persisted. This resulted only in frustration on my part with no additional information gained about Devon. Additional consultation with Devon's mother, as well as with my supervisor, helped me begin to recognize the need to go beyond using questions with young children.

Looking back, I see that I needed to accept Devon's difficult temperament and work with it, not against it. Experience has taught me that treatment must be based on a child's natural disposition to be effective. The following are step-by-step guidelines for adapting your initial interview with children of varying temperaments.

Easy-Tempered Kids

Children with easy temperaments will likely be fairly comfortable upon meeting you. However, their friendly disposition also means that they may be very concerned with behaving "appropriately." These kids need to know that there are virtually no rules about or limits on what can be discussed in session. When explaining treatment, be sure to include statements that highlight the accepting and permissive nature of therapy:

> "Some kids think they need to 'behave' or be 'nice' in here and not talk about certain things. But this is a place where anything can be talked about, even things many adults think are not respectful or appropriate. My job is to get to know what kids think, feel, and wonder about as much as possible so I can really understand them. It may take a while, but over time, kids share things with me that are really hard to say to other adults. When they do, some things in life can be better, like feeling less worried or scared."

Difficult-Tempered Kids

Children with difficult temperaments will likely be poorly regulated, which means they will often immediately begin exploring your office or playroom. Making one invitation to sit and converse may be worthwhile, but more as a way to observe their ability to cooperate rather than to engage them in significant dialogue. Allow these active kids to roam, and have some "fiddle objects" on hand to occupy them long enough for you to explain the basics of therapy. Keep the explanation short—you can give them additional information bit by bit over the course of the session.

In addition, be ready to set limits, especially on which areas of the room are okay and not okay to explore. Many difficult children will want to engage in more intense or possibly aggressive play. Be ready to redirect any aggressive play to action figures, a punching bag (I use a weighted canvas wrestling bag), or a pull-apart doll. Do not allow aggression toward you unless it is symbolic. (For example, a toy gun pointed at you is acceptable, but putting the gun against your forehead is not.)

Slow-to-Warm-Up Kids

Slow-to-warm-up children are the ones most likely to wear their anxiety on their sleeve. During your initial interview with these kids, I recommend following one basic rule: Don't try too hard. These highly perceptive kids will sense that you want to talk with them, but they likely won't be ready to do so in this first session. Instead, spend more time talking with the parent who accompanies them into your office (preferably only during the first few minutes of the first session).

Avoid making directives or requests early on. Instead, begin by describing the contents of the room and talking about your role as a therapist. However, do so with your one-step-removed approach, rather than referring directly to them:

> "When kids come here, they are allowed to talk, play, and draw however they like. My job is to get to know them. They can talk as little or as much as they like."

Give these kids more specific information on the typical sequence of events during a first session, such as when you will bring them back to the waiting room to see their parents. Next, give them permission to talk or not talk, explore the room, or draw. Assure them that it's okay to be unsure at first, then state that kids start to feel more comfortable as they get used to being there. The goal in this first session is not a considerable amount of conversation; rather, it's achieving any kind of positive interchange that doesn't add to the child's anxiety, as well as keen observation. If the child does speak with you during the first session, that's a bonus!

Creative Corner

- Provide art materials for slow-to-warm-up kids and gross motor play items, like punching bags, for difficult-tempered kids.
- Commenting on their art/play process will prove more useful than seated conversation.

TREATMENT HIGHLIGHTS

- Educate parents about the role the brain plays in their child's anxiety.

- Take children on a journey through the brain.

- Assist kids in developing individualized relaxation strategies.

- Provide parents with information on temperament and goodness of fit.

- Use temperament-informed approaches, especially in the beginning of treatment.

CHAPTER 3

Healthy Habits: Caring for the Body to Calm the Mind

We all know that taking good care of our bodies leads not only to better physical health, but also better mental health. However, establishing and maintaining healthy lifestyle habits for kids and families is often precluded by hectic work and school schedules, domestic necessities, and numerous other time demands. To cope with such stress, kids and parents alike may resort to excessive device usage, which can easily become a form of chronic distraction or escapism that interferes with maintaining healthy daily habits.

The handouts, worksheets, and treatment tips in this chapter are designed to help kids and their families assess obstacles to a healthier lifestyle. You can start by suggesting simple, gradual changes to modify current less healthy habits, then move on to providing guidance for building on these changes to create long-term healthy lifestyle habits.

The Critical Trio: Eating, Sleeping, and Movement

Research shows that a healthy diet, consistent sleep, and regular exercise are three critical components of a lower-stress lifestyle that can help alleviate or deescalate anxiety. Developing and maintaining these healthy habits is most successful when families do it together in a scheduled, moderate, and consistent manner (Trigueros et al., 2022).

Healthy Eating for Less Anxiety

A diet rich in complex carbohydrates (e.g., oatmeal and whole grains), lean protein, fruit, vegetables, and legumes, as well as plenty of water, helps our anxiety levels be more manageable. Specifically, steering clear of highly processed and sugary foods helps our bodies maintain more stable blood sugar levels, which tends to reduce anxiety. Processed meats, fried foods, high-fat dairy products, and of course caffeine have all been shown to contribute to anxiety (Saneei et al., 2016).

Taking Inventory of Your Kitchen

This worksheet will help you identify the types of foods you bring into your family's household. Draw check marks to indicate how often you purchase each item:

√√√ Consistently buy   √√ Often buy   √ Rarely buy   Never buy

If there are other items you purchase that aren't listed, write these in the blank spaces within their appropriate categories.

When you have finished, use the information you discover to start reducing your family's consumption of processed or sugary foods and increasing your consumption of whole/unprocessed foods. Take a moment to consider what healthier options you can substitute for the less healthy foods your kids (and perhaps you) crave.

I. Boxed Items	II. Dairy	III. Vegetables
____ Cookies	____ Whole milk	____ Fresh vegetables
____ Crackers	____ Low-fat/skim milk	____ Frozen vegetables
____ Chips/cheese crisps	____ Cream	____ Canned vegetables
____ Pretzels	____ Cheese	
____ Granola/snack bars/cakes	____ Ice cream	
____ Pancake/waffle/cake mixes	____ Yogurt	
____ Cereal		
IV. Meat	**V. Seafood**	**VI. Grains**
____ Ground beef/sirloin	____ Fresh seafood	____ White bread/rolls/buns
____ Steak	____ Fresh-frozen seafood	____ Wheat/rye bread
____ Pork	____ Processed/frozen seafood (e.g., fish sticks)	____ Oatmeal (plain)
____ Chicken		____ Oatmeal (processed)
____ Turkey		

Improved Sleep for Less Anxiety

We live in a sleep-deprived society. According to the Centers for Disease Control and Prevention (2022), a third of adults in the US are not getting enough sleep on a regular basis. It's even worse when it comes to our children—almost half of kids in the US don't get the recommended 9 hours of sleep, and 10 percent have a significant sleep issue. This rises to 50 percent or more in children with mental health or neurodevelopmental disorders.

Sleep-deprived kids tend to have more behavioral problems, health issues, and challenges with anxiety and mood (Taveras et al., 2017). Moreover, children who do not obtain sufficient sleep are more at risk for neurocognitive problems in early adolescence (Yang et al., 2022). Additional research by psychologist Jean Twenge (2020) reveals that frequent device usage is another major contributing factor to sleep deprivation; the ongoing stimulus of online activity prevents our brains from settling down enough for sound and sufficient sleep.

Anxiety itself often contributes to sleeping problems. Many kids and adults worry or are fearful at bedtime, making sleep more challenging. Considering the connection between poor sleep and increased anxiety, it's only natural that a cycle of sleep deprivation and anxiety can develop over time.

However it comes about, sleep deprivation makes reducing anxiety an even greater uphill battle, so be sure to address the issue of sleep with the kids and families you serve.

TIPS WITH TEENS

- FOMO (fear of missing out) is a major obstacle to adolescents' sleep quality. Help them develop a method for buffering themselves from device usage during sleeping hours.

- Encourage teens to limit use of devices that emit blue light (phones, television, gaming devices, etc.) one hour before bed and find alternative activities that promote relaxation and calm.

- Gently explore how their daily diet and movement may help or hinder sleep *without* sounding parental. For example, "I bet you already know that healthy eating and exercise can improve sleep a lot. You certainly don't need another adult telling you what to do. However, if you ever want to discuss your daily habits, let me know."

How Sleep-Friendly Is Our Household?

The right environment is critical for obtaining proper sleep. Determine how sleep-friendly your household is by considering the following statements. Rate each item on a scale of 1 to 5, where 1 = strongly disagree, 2 = somewhat disagree, 3 = unsure, 4 = agree, and 5 = strongly agree.

_____ Bedtime is well-established and consistent for the kids in our household.

_____ Bedtime is well-established and consistent for the adults in our household.

_____ My child's bedroom is conducive for good sleep: adequately dark, cool, comfortable, and quiet.

_____ My bedroom is conducive for good sleep: adequately dark, cool, comfortable, and quiet.

_____ When the kids are in bed, the rest of the household is reasonably quiet.

_____ Electronic devices are not in the children's rooms after bedtime.

_____ Televisions are either not in the children's rooms or are unable to be turned on after bedtime.

_____ Our family has a nightly routine for instilling relaxation and preparing for bed.

Add all your ratings together. If your total score is below 30, consider what changes you can make to improve sleep quality in your household.

How Can I Get Better Sleep?

Studies show that we need good sleep for our bodies and minds to work well. Good sleep also helps us be less anxious. Finish the following sentences to figure out what changes you and your parents can make so you can become a super sleeper!

1. Something that would relax me before bedtime would be _____

   _____.

2. My bedroom would be more comfy if _____

   _____.

3. Something I can do by myself when I'm nervous or scared in my bed is _____

   _____.

4. If my bedroom was less _____

   and more _____, I would sleep better.

5. Maybe my parents can help me sleep better by _____

   _____.

6. If I'm worried about something at bedtime, I can _____

   _____.

7. When I have a bad dream, I can go back to sleep if I _____

   _____.

8. My parents don't know that I don't sleep well when they _____

   _____.

Movement and Exercise for Less Anxiety

Research has shown that exercise can improve mental health by strengthening the brain's ability to manage stress. It has also shown that regular exercise allows people with insomnia to fall asleep faster, sleep longer, and obtain better quality sleep. Some researchers found that people who exercised regularly were 25 percent less likely to develop depression or an anxiety disorder over the next five years. Just five minutes of aerobic exercise each day can be enough to produce anti-anxiety effects (Otto & Smits, 2011).

Regular exercise has become even more critical to our well-being with the onslaught of technological conveniences and amusements that make our lifestyles increasingly sedentary. Children in particular don't get adequate physical activity in our modern world. The age at which physical activity drops off for most kids is younger than experts originally thought: Recent research shows that many children's activity levels drop considerably and their sedentary behaviors begin to increase at age eight (Schwarzfischer et al., 2019).

Promoting Physical Activity

In today's often sedentary world, getting our bodies moving is more important than ever. Here are some tips for increasing your child's physical activity level:

1. Be a physically active role model.

2. Get around by walking and biking whenever possible.

3. Exercise routinely as a family.

4. Focus on fun and creativity; be silly.

5. Invite your child's friends to join you in outdoor adventures and other fun movement activities.

6. Create games that promote cooperation.

7. Give active chore options such as vacuuming or raking leaves.

8. Give gifts that encourage exercise, such as a bicycle, skateboard, or jump rope.

9. Integrate "no-tech times" into the daily schedule.

10. Plan family outings and vacations around outdoor activities.

Assisting Families With Developing Healthier Habits

While lifestyle changes are often essential for promoting mental wellness and improving anxiety management, such changes can feel overwhelming for busy, stressed-out families. Remember, significant change is best accomplished gradually, with plenty of support along the way. Consider the following step-by-step method for promoting healthier lifestyle habits for anxious kids and families:

1. Assess the following *before* any attempts at changing lifestyle habits:

   • Each family member's readiness, motivation, and resistance to healthier habits

   • Psychosocial stressors, obstacles, and challenges to making healthy changes

   • Details about their current habits and routines around eating, exercise, sleeping, and so forth

2. Empower children and parents to select one small, specific change to implement.

3. Assist families in identifying potential sabotage factors and preparing a prevention plan.

4. Establish reassessment dates for evaluating progress and making additional changes.

TREATMENT HIGHLIGHTS

• Before discussing any potential lifestyle changes, assess the child and family's current health habits.

• Determine readiness for change, keeping in mind the family's current stress level and priorities.

• Collaborate with the parents and child to select one small change (in diet, sleep, or exercise) to commit to for a specified time period. When the period has ended, reassess and make modifications as needed.

• Gradually discuss and add other changes as progress is made.

CHAPTER 4

Life at Home: Lowering the Temperature and Slowing the Pace

All too often, families today have tension-filled, high-stress lifestyles that move at a mile a minute: Get up, prepare for the day, perform at school or work, return home, begin homework and chores, then dinner, more homework and chores, bedtime (often a battle) . . . and the cycle repeats the next day.

A higher degree of household stress is associated with increased anxiety and disruptive behavior in young children (Fields et al., 2021). In order to have a significant impact in our efforts to help kids with anxiety, we must examine the emotional climate of the household. I often collaborate with parents and kids to find ways to lower the "temperature" and moderate the pace of family life. Helping these families slow down and better manage frustration and conflict is key for combating anxiety.

Adjusting the Emotional Thermostat

> "I don't like it when my parents yell at me."

As child therapists, we often hear this remark from the anxious kids. Frustrated parents believe they must become loud and angry to get cooperation from their children—"They only listen to me when I yell!" is the rationale. We must assist parents and kids in breaking this cycle by providing practical guidance for how they approach and communicate with each other. Otherwise, the emotional temperature of the household remains too high, which can keep both kids and parents in a state of tension.

Defusing Chronic Discord in Parental Styles

> "You are way too harsh with him."

> "Well, you baby him beyond belief."

We often hear accusations like these from parents who have highly discrepant styles. *Polarized parenting* (Pendry & Adam, 2007) like this occurs when a permissive parent and an authoritarian parent battle over the child's emotional and behavioral challenges, whether it be how to address those challenges or who is responsible for causing or aggravating them. While such conflict can occur in any family, it is particularly common in divorced and blended family situations.

A critical component for defusing chronic parental style discord is to highlight that each parent has a valid point, while also pointing out that their opposing styles intensify household tension and likely strengthen or at least sustain their child's anxiety. Since this idea may be difficult for parents to hear (especially those who tend to be fragile or defensive), I typically convey it using *positive pseudo-assumptions*. For example:

> "I know that both of you want Liam to be less anxious and more cooperative. I also know that you realize how your conflict contributes to his anxiety—something that I know that neither of you wants to happen."

Teaching Parents to Enter Their Child's "Bubble"

Most parents don't enjoy yelling, and they often feel powerless, guilty, or exhausted afterward. It typically starts with a simple and necessary directive, such as "Wash up, get dressed, and come downstairs for breakfast." But because the parents are often pressed for time, they communicate the directives quickly and in passing, an approach I call "walk-bys." Time goes by with no response from the child, and another walk-by directive is issued, louder this time. You see where this is going.

The first step in breaking the yelling cycle is to assist parents with creating more time for themselves. This may mean doing more preparation the night before (with the kids' help, where appropriate) and getting up earlier. I encourage parents to bear in mind when approaching their child that the child is often in their own bubble, engrossed in an activity or deep in a thought process or state of mind. No directive should be given until the parent gently enters the child's bubble by learning and acknowledging what the child is doing or thinking at the moment:

> "Hey Mateo. What are you up to right now? Oh yeah, that's cool! So, I need your attention for a moment—ready? I need you to stop what you're doing for now and start getting dressed. I'll leave the room as soon as you get started."

Help parents understand that by taking the extra time to enter the bubble and not leaving the room until the transition begins, the odds of cooperation are much higher and the chance for conflict lower. If cooperation still isn't adequate, then the parent should repeat the process, with an added mention of how the child can choose to cooperate or not, and that lack of cooperation will bring a consequence. (Ideally, the parent should already have a practical and appropriate consequence in mind.) The key is for the parent to maintain an empowered but calm presence. I remind parents that they are teaching their kids cause and effect, which is much more valuable than simply teaching compliance.

Say It Versus Show It

Parents are only human, and they are certainly entitled to feeling frustrated, irritated, and angry. However, when negative emotions are intensely displayed, anxious children become more anxious, which leads them to shut down or act out. In moments where emotions are heightening, I encourage parents to *say it versus show it.* When they identify how they are feeling to their children, the emotional intensity remains level while feelings and needs are still communicated:

> "Lydia, I've asked you to pick up your clothes and you agreed to do so, but they are still on the floor. I am really frustrated about that, and I'm starting to get angry."

Slowing the Pace With Smoother Transitions

> "Get up … get dressed … get moving … let's go!"

From home to school to after-school activities, a hectic pace seems like the norm these days. But is it healthy? For kids prone to anxiety, the answer is no. For many kids, there is barely time to take a breath between one task ending and the next beginning.

While life does require us to move quickly at times, I encourage parents to be mindful about just how fast they're expecting their kids to transition from one activity to another. Kids with anxiety tend to require more notice of a transition, and more time to adjust to it. I recommend that parents break down transitions into three parts:

1. **The preview:** "In about ten minutes, I'm going to ask you to stop gaming and change clothes to go to Grandma's house."

2. **Initial assistance:** "Okay, it's time to get dressed. How can I help you get started?"

3. **The follow-up:** "I'm back, so that means it's time to leave. Anything else I can help you with?"

Over time, the parents' assistance can gradually fade as the child becomes more capable of transitioning independently. I remind parents that this can be a slow process. If progress isn't occurring, a more significant anxiety issue may be at play, such as generalized anxiety disorder or obsessive-compulsive disorder. Later chapters will address these challenges.

Morning and Evening Relaxation Rituals

Another way to slow the pace of family life is to assist kids and families in developing brief routines or rituals: one to begin the day in a relaxed but energized state, and one to facilitate a more restful type of relaxation before bedtime. This might involve a morning stretch to a favorite song or a few deep breaths while tensing and releasing muscle groups from head to toe, and in the evening, a warm beverage while listening to calming music or a warm bath and a story. With young children, these rituals work best if the whole family participates. Older kids may need some help in creating routines that aren't too stimulating. (In case it needs to be said, gaming would be a poor choice.)

Creative Corner

Running a household can be serious business. We must help parents infuse the power of play and humor into their daily schedules. Turning chores into games and adding a touch of silliness to boring routines can do a lot to reduce household stress that contributes to anxiety.

Guidelines for Calmer Communication

When asking your child to perform a task . . .

1. **Observe.** Notice the current behavior of your child.

2. **Greet.** Say hello to simply make your presence known.

3. **Comment.** "Looks like you're really into that game!"

4. **Request attention.** "Can you please take a short break? I need your help."

5. **State the directive.** "I need you to get ready for our dinner out with your grandparents."

6. **Provide a five-minute wrap-up.** If necessary, state you will return in five minutes.

7. **Follow up.** If no progress has been made, ask again for cooperation and state a consequence if the child refuses: "I need you to get ready for dinner. If you choose not to do this, you will lose game privileges for the rest of the evening."

8. **Remain with them.** Allow two minutes for your child to decide whether to cooperate or experience a consequence.

9. **Follow through.** Either express appreciation for their cooperation or follow through with the consequence for noncompliance.

Starting and Ending My Day in a Relaxed Way

Morning and evening routines are very important for starting your day in a calm, focused way and ending your day as peaceful and relaxed as possible.

1. Think about how your day begins and ends—are there parts that can be stressful?

   » In the morning I get stressed out when _____

   _____.

   » When it's almost time for bed, I can get stressed when _____

   _____.

2. What changes could you make in the morning so you can start your day off relaxed and more focused?

   » My day will start off better if I begin the day by _____

   _____.

3. What could you do differently before bedtime so that you can wind down, relax, and get a good night's sleep?

   » My day will end in a relaxing way if I end my day before bed by _____

   _____.

TREATMENT HIGHLIGHTS

- Assess the emotional climate of the child's household. This means determining the level of family tension/conflict and how often high-intensity communication occurs.

- Determine the level of structure that the family follows on a daily basis. Both excessive, inflexible schedules and minimally structured schedules can promote anxiety.

- Recognize how a combination of permissive and authoritarian parenting styles can result in a chronic cycle of parental conflict. Help each parent lean in the other direction regarding their style.

- Collaborate with parents on strategies to make morning and evening transitions more time efficient and less stressful.

- Teach and model lower-intensity communication via the *say it versus show it* approach.

CHAPTER 5

Mindfulness: De-Stressing in an Overstimulating World

Mindfulness has become a bit of a buzzword over the past decade or so, but no one can deny its importance, especially in stressful times. Mindfulness is a mental state achieved by focusing on the present moment while accepting thoughts, feelings, and bodily sensations as they arise. At its core, mindfulness is a form of meditation that requires practice and utilizes breathing, guided imagery, and other methods for relaxing and de-stressing both body and mind.

In our overly wired world, mindfulness is needed more than ever. Excessive technology usage can contribute to stress, conflict, and health problems, and the practice of mindfulness is key for resetting our overscheduled, overstimulated brains. In particular, the therapeutic application of mindfulness for children and their parents is fundamental to anxiety treatment. Research shows that mindfulness has significant psychological and physical benefits that promote more effective anxiety management (Shapiro & Weisbaum, 2020). Simply stated, mindfulness serves as a tool for resetting an over-anxious mind.

I believe mindfulness should be viewed as a lifestyle habit, like healthy eating or exercise, that can be taught to children just like other healthy habits—the earlier, the better. However, this requires the adults in their lives to practice and model mindfulness on a regular basis.

> Incorporating mindfulness into our own lives as clinicians will not only improve our own well-being but also better prepare us to integrate mindfulness into our clinical work.

Effective Device Management

Device preoccupation has become a monumental challenge in the world of parenting. Research shows that excessive device usage correlates with increased anxiety and depression (Al Salman et al., 2020), yet preventing kids from using devices is both impractical and virtually (pun intended) impossible. In fact, attempts to block device usage altogether can create anxiety in itself, typically leading to intense parent-child conflict.

Unfortunately, there are no quick and easy answers to this digital dilemma. A practical place to start is asking questions that help you understand the daily patterns of each family member's technology usage. The more specific information you collect, the better. How much usage involves gaming, social media, texting, specific apps, streaming, and so on? Be sure to include technology usage of all kinds, including schoolwork and parents' work from home.

Once you've learned the patterns of daily usage, focus your questions around the antecedents and outcomes of this usage—what occurs in the family environment right before, during, and after the use of various technologies? Again, collect specifics on the negative interchanges between family members that directly relate to device usage. These insights will help you know when, where, and how to intervene effectively.

Finally, bring the parents and kids together to collaboratively develop a device schedule with both limits and flexibility. Having a few options provides kids with some sense of control. It is crucial for both parents to agree on this tentative schedule before approaching children with it. I recommend a schedule that includes times when technology can always be used *and* times when it can never be used ("no-tech times"). Emphasize that the schedule will work best if the entire family adheres to it as much as possible (especially the no-tech times). Bear in mind that because most kids and teens do not yet have adequate ability to regulate their device usage, devices must *not* be accessible during no-tech times.

CASE EXAMPLE: Device Usage

Parents Tom and Maria are exasperated with 13-year-old Sofia's constant attachment to her phone. They report that she is seldom seen without the phone in her hand, engrossed in "her own little world." In fact, Tom and Maria note that Sofia stays in her room most of the time and seems uninterested in seeing her friends face-to-face. Their attempts to wean her off the phone, especially to do homework, chores, and dinner preparation, have only resulted in yelling matches.

After obtaining specifics on the device usage of the entire family as well as the when, where, and how of negative interchanges around it, I focus on determining the parents' expectations. What do Tom and Maria deem appropriate and manageable device usage on weekdays? How about on the weekend? What do they each think about their own and their partner's technology use? How consistent are their expectations of Sofia—do one or both of them tend to vary in how they monitor or respond to her usage?

My next step involves helping Tom and Maria devise a tentative device usage schedule for Sofia with some options to give her a sense of control. Once they both agree on this schedule, I encourage them to first approach Sofia with just the *idea* of developing a device usage schedule together. Obtaining her initial preference is important to avoid her seeing the schedule as being imposed upon her. After speaking with Sofia, they can further consult with each other to modify this initial schedule they've made.

Finally, I instruct them to obtain Sofia's feedback on the revised schedule and, if necessary, to collaborate with her in modifying the schedule one more time. I add a caution to be realistic in their expectations in this process, understanding that any such schedule will likely not be totally satisfactory to her (nor, possibly, to the parents). I encourage follow-up parent sessions to assess how the schedule is working and assist in making changes with input from all parties.

The Needs Behind the Screens

While a structured but somewhat flexible device usage schedule is necessary and helpful, its effectiveness will be limited unless you explore the psychological needs being met by such usage.

Today's kids are often termed *digital natives* due to having grown up around smartphones and other devices. For children today, virtual *is* their reality; the basic social-emotional needs driving them— recognition, acceptance, belonging, validation of their self-worth and attractiveness, and so forth—are just as relevant online as they are offline (if not more so). In fact, kids from Generation Alpha (born in 2010 and later) have an especially high need to express their identity online, often in a manner strikingly consistent with modes of corporate branding.

Helping parents understand these psychological needs is critical to helping kids get these needs met in a variety of healthy, nonvirtual ways. Device usage cannot be reduced unless it's replaced by real-life activities and experiences. Collaborate with both the child and parents to come up with other activities that could meet the same needs as the device usage. Encourage further discussion, with your help as needed, that can help the child select one activity to start using as a partial substitute for some of the device usage time.

Mindfulness as the Path From Virtual Reality to Real Life

While technology usage can threaten mindfulness, it can also assist it to a degree. An increasing number of apps exist to support mindfulness practices such as meditation, deep breathing, and body scanning. Such apps may be particularly helpful with teens, who may be more resistant to reducing their technology usage. There are also a growing number of books for teaching children mindfulness. One of my favorites is *Mindfulness for Children* by Uz Afzal (2018), which includes lots of child-friendly mindfulness activities.

TIPS WITH TEENS

- Explore technological ways to promote mindfulness, such as mindfulness-based instructional videos and apps.

- Encourage teens to develop and share mindfulness tips with their anxious friends.

- Suggest teens gradually ease into more "monotasking" rather than multitasking for activities and responsibilities that require greater focus.

Practice Kindness for Mindfulness

Want to become better at mindfulness? Practice kindness! Being kind to yourself and others is really important for becoming less anxious. Answer the following questions to discover how you can become a kinder and more mindful person.

1. When I look in the mirror, a kind thought about myself could be _____

   _____

   _____ .

2. When I notice something different about someone else, it would be kind to think _____

   _____

   _____ .

3. When I make a mistake, a kind thing to tell myself would be _____

   _____

   _____ .

4. When someone else makes a mistake, a kind thing I could say would be _____

   _____

   _____ .

5. When I do something I shouldn't have done at home or school, a kind thing I can try to think is

   _____

   _____ .

6. When I see someone else get in trouble at home or school, I could be kind by _____

   _____

   _____ .

Overcoming Obstacles to Mindfulness

As a busy parent, it can be challenging to focus on the present moment rather than on the many responsibilities and tasks on your to-do list. Completing the following sentences will help you begin to develop strategies for learning to live in the moment with greater calm, focus, and intention.

1. In the mornings, I tend to be preoccupied with _____
   _____.

   I can be calmer while still being productive by focusing more on _____
   _____.

2. Much of my energy during the day goes toward _____
   _____.

   To feel more calm and present, I can begin redirecting some of that energy toward _____
   _____.

3. I have a tendency to be distracted by _____
   _____,

   especially when I need to _____
   _____.

   One way to reduce or manage this distraction might be _____
   _____.

4. In the evenings, I am often preoccupied with _____
   _____.

   I can become more relaxed by focusing more on _____
   _____.

Building Your Mindfulness Muscle

Becoming more mindful takes practice. The good news is that you can practice mindfulness while doing activities that you already do every day. Here are some ideas for practicing mindfulness throughout your day.

1. **When you wake up in the morning:**

   » Notice how your toothpaste tastes and how the bristles of the toothbrush feel as you brush your teeth.

   » Pay attention to the temperature of the water and the texture of the soap as you wash your face and shower or bathe.

   » How does your shampoo feel and smell as you wash your hair? How does the towel feel against your skin as you dry off?

2. **When you are eating:**

   » How does your food smell? Is the smell pleasant or not so much?

   » How does the food feel in your mouth? Is it smooth or grainy?

   » How does your food taste? Is it sweet, salty, yummy, or bland?

   » Are you eating slowly enough to notice when you're becoming full?

3. **When you are walking outside:**

   » How does the sun, rain, or wind feel against your skin?

   » Do you notice anything that is very colorful?

   » What sounds do you hear?

4. **When you're in bed:**

   » How do your sheets, pillow, and blanket feel?

   » What thoughts are in your mind?

   » What can you focus on to become calm and relaxed?

TREATMENT HIGHLIGHTS

- Integrate mindfulness into your work with children and families. Incorporating mindfulness into your own life is a great place to start and will only enhance your clinical effectiveness.

- Highlight the anxiety-reducing benefits of practicing mindfulness as a family for both anxious children and their parents.

- Recognize how excessive device usage can interfere with developing and practicing mindfulness.

- Assess each family member's device usage, as well as the associated interpersonal events, before assisting with any device usage schedules.

- Guide parents in collaborating on a device usage schedule that gives kids some level of input and control.

- Help kids and their families gradually replace device time with real-life activities and experiences that meet the same psychological needs.

CHAPTER 6

The 3 R's of Anxiety Management: Recognize, Relax, and Redirect

When kids are in the throes of anxiety, sympathetic adults often attempt to calm them with reassurance and reason:

"You're okay."

"Everything's fine."

"There's nothing to be scared of."

"You've handled this situation before, remember?"

Frustrated adults often resort to a rather forceful approach:

"Enough of this nonsense!"

"You're being ridiculous!"

"Just *stop* it!"

"If you don't knock it off, there will be consequences."

Finally, highly empathic adults may enable avoidance:

"I know you're frightened, so we can just try this another day."

"It's okay. Stop crying. You can stay here with us."

"I'm so sorry—I didn't mean to upset you. Do you want to go home?"

None of these methods are very effective. In fact, they are likely to only exacerbate a child's anxiety. However, by understanding the effects of anxiety on a child's brain, we can better respond to children who are in a heightened state of arousal.

When a child's anxiety peaks, their brain is in survival mode—the amygdala has triggered the child to either fight, flee, or freeze. I sometimes remind parents that it's impossible to reason with or coerce the cortex when the amygdala is essentially "on fire." Allowing the child to avoid or escape the feared situation will temporarily calm the amygdala, but doing so reinforces their perception of danger.

I encourage parents to avoid avoidance—it is anxiety's best friend! Lasting relief from anxiety is only possible as the child grasps the reality that they are safe from harm.

One of my goals when working with anxious children and their parents is to make anxiety-management strategies easy to remember. Borrowing from a combination of psychoeducation, relaxation, and cognitive-behavioral approaches, I teach children and caretakers the "3 R's" of anxiety management: *recognize*, *relax*, and *redirect*.

What's Really Happening?
Recognizing What Anxiety Is and Isn't

Children often give their anxiety a lot of meaning. They think, *If I'm feeling like this, something really bad is about to happen.* For example, if a child experiences stomach discomfort, they assume, *I must be sick* or *I'm going to throw up!* Therefore, it's important to help children recognize what anxiety actually is and what it isn't. Here is an example of what I tell kids to help them understand what's happening when they feel anxious:

> "Anxiety means that your body is making your usual brain chemicals that we all have, but it's making too much—so much that it causes a 'flood' and overflows into different parts of your body. The good news is this flood isn't dangerous. However, the flood makes us *think* we are in danger. Sometimes the flood makes you think terrible things will happen to yourself or those you care about. The flood can also make parts of your body feel bad, like a headache or stomachache. The brain chemical flood can feel really scary, especially when it makes you think or feel like you can't breathe or even convinces you that you're going to die. All this makes it really hard to stay calm! It's important to remember that even though anxiety can make you feel really bad or unsafe, it doesn't have the power to actually harm you."

I then help kids recognize the mental, emotional, and physiological signs of their anxiety: How does their anxiety flood show itself? Do they experience racing thoughts, catastrophizing, intense worry or fear, shortness of breath, or stomach pain? (For more possible signals, see the Signs of Anxiety in Kids worksheet, p. 28.) The most important part is helping kids grasp that all of these thoughts, feelings, and body sensations mean *nothing* except that their brain is being flooded with chemicals that are causing anxiety and thus creating these symptoms.

Once the child understands what anxiety looks and feels like in their mind and body, they can start to identify when they tend to experience anxiety. This helps them to both anticipate situations that could lead to increased anxiety and recognize their symptoms in the moment. The more they learn about when and how their anxiety acts up, the better they become at recognizing when it's time to relax and redirect.

"I Need to Chill": Discovering the Child's Favorite *Relaxation* Techniques

The second *R* refers to strategies for slowing down the child's central nervous system and promoting a calmer state. Children can learn a variety of relaxation methods, such as deep breathing, mindfulness-based practices, visualization, muscle tensing and releasing, and empowering self-talk (refer to chapter 5).

Children tend to have preferred ways to relax depending on their learning style. For example, visual learners prefer using their imagination to picture a peaceful scene, auditory learners prefer soothing music, and tactile learners find soft or smooth textures to be most relaxing. Regardless of the technique, relaxation is key to anxiety management because the cortex can only function properly once the amygdala is adequately soothed. Assisting parents with learning how best to attend to their child's physiological state is critical, since many parents inadvertently overlook the relaxation step and jump straight to talking, often at length, in an unsuccessful attempt to soothe the child.

Time to *Redirect*: Action Plans and Distraction

Finally, the third *R* involves teaching the child to channel their thoughts and behaviors in positive and productive ways. Redirection takes one of two forms: an action plan or a distraction.

Action plans are advisable when the child's anxiety has an element of realism and some kind of action can be taken to alleviate it. For example, if a child's anxiety takes the form of intense worry about an upcoming test, an action plan can be developed, such as planning times to study.

If the child's anxiety has little to no basis in reality or if the anxiety is about something over which the child has no control, then distraction is a better option. If a child is preoccupied about her father potentially being in an airplane accident while traveling for work, an effective strategy might be helping the child find a healthy distraction, such as playing a game, calling a friend, or watching a movie. Note that it is critical for recognition and relaxation to *precede* the use of redirection. Otherwise, children may learn to only use distraction as a means of coping, which can prevent them from developing effective self-soothing and relaxation skills.

The following pages in this chapter contain various activities for assisting children in applying the 3 R's of anxiety management. Remember that it's also critical to teach parents this approach so the skills can be practiced and reinforced at home and elsewhere. Many parents find the 3 R's helpful in managing their own anxiety as well, which further enhances their skill in parenting and their sense of competence.

The 3 R's of Anxiety Management

Anytime you begin to feel scared, nervous, worried, like you can't breathe, or like your stomach hurts, remember to use the **3 R's**. Try to use these three steps as soon as you feel uncomfortable. If you forget or are having trouble doing it alone, ask your parent or another adult for help by saying something like, "I need help using the 3 R's." You might also want to post this handout in your house where you can easily see it as a reminder to use the 3 R's whenever you begin to feel anxious.

Remember, managing anxiety takes practice, just like any skill or sport. Make this one of your healthy habits, and you will definitely get better at it over time!

1. **RECOGNIZE the signs of anxiety.**

   » "That's my anxiety. My brain is making too many of those chemicals again."

   » "My anxious feelings do not mean something bad is definitely going to happen; it just *feels* that way."

2. **RELAX to calm your body and mind.**

   » "Time to take a few slow, deep breaths. Breathe in through my nose and out through my mouth."

   » "I'm going to do some nice, slow stretches. Reach up high, then reach down low."

   » "I can use my imagination to see myself in any place that relaxes me."

   » "Maybe I can find something that smells or feels nice, or I can listen to calm music."

3. **REDIRECT to an action plan or distraction.**

   » "I can come up with a plan on my own."

   » "I'm not sure if I can make a plan for this, so I'll ask a family member."

   » "I can't think of a plan, so I need to get my brain or body busy with something interesting, challenging, or fun!"

Using the 3 R's of Anxiety Management With Your Child

Your child's anxiety can be very persistent. It's understandable for you to be concerned but also frustrated, even irritated, given how often you are approached with the same worry, fear, question, or physical symptom. While it's helpful to acknowledge your child's concern and empathize with them, avoid asking them "why" or giving a lengthy explanation about it. As you know, these tactics seldom work. In fact, too much discussion about the content of a child's anxiety can actually strengthen it. Instead, guide them through the **3 R's** of anxiety management.

1. **RECOGNIZE your child's anxiety signals.**
   - » Physical complaints: Headache, stomachache, tight chest, choking sensation
   - » Thought/fear complaints: "I'm scared a robber is going to break in"
   - » Repetitive/what-if questions: "What if I die in my sleep?"

   Your response: "That's a scary thought. You know that comes from anxiety. It means you've got some extra brain chemicals going on right now."

2. **RELAX your child's body.**

   After helping your child recognize the anxiety, encourage and model:
   - » Slow, deep breathing
   - » Positive self-talk: "We can breathe through this anxiety"
   - » Stretching
   - » Finding soothing smells, sounds/music, or textures

3. **REDIRECT toward a plan or distraction.**

   For anxiety about something that is based in reality and that is within your child's control, mutually develop a plan of action.
   - » Example: "What if I fail my math test?"
   - » Your response: "Let's make a study schedule so you'll be ready"

   For anxiety about something that is unrealistic or outside of your child's control, help your child find an enjoyable distraction.
   - » Example: "What if someone kidnaps you, Mom?"
   - » Your response: "Let's play a game," "I need some help in the kitchen," "What should we do for Dad's birthday?"

When Does My Anxiety Show Itself?

Complete the following statements to learn about when your anxiety tends to show itself. The more you learn about when and how your anxiety acts up, the better you will become at knowing when it's time to relax and redirect!

1. My body feels uncomfortable when _____
   _____.

2. I feel most scared when _____
   _____.

3. I notice that my _____ feels _____
   when _____.

4. I don't like it when I think about _____
   _____.

5. I worry most when _____
   _____.

6. It's very frustrating whenever _____
   _____.

7. I get weird feelings in my stomach when _____
   _____.

8. It's really hard not to think about _____
   _____.

9. My heart or chest feels tight when _____
   _____.

10. I tend to cry when _____
    _____.

How Can the 3 R's Benefit Me and My Child?

As a parent of a child with anxiety, you have likely experienced some anxiety yourself—most parents would! As your child learns to use the 3 R's of anxiety management, take a moment to complete the following statements for yourself. After reflecting on how you express anxiety, consider how you can use the 3 R's to improve your own well-being. Anxious kids are especially sensitive to their parents' emotional states, so being a good self-regulator creates a win-win—you experience less anxiety, and as a result, so does your child!

1. When I become anxious, I often tend to _____

_____.

2. I tend to feel tension in my _____ and pain or

discomfort in my _____.

3. My anxiety-based thoughts often take the form of _____

_____.

4. I have a tendency to become preoccupied with _____

_____.

5. I have been told that I need to _____

_____.

6. I will start practicing more relaxation by _____

_____.

7. I feel productive and a sense of relief when I _____

_____.

8. I'm going to add more fun and healthy distraction to my life by _____

_____.

Additional Considerations When Using the 3 R's

Recognition

The first recognizable sign of anxiety is often physiological, emotional, or cognitive, depending on the child. Children differ as to which signals they notice—it's typically either the one that causes the most distress or the one that allows them to avoid the feared situation. Begin recognition awareness by first focusing on the most obvious signal while gradually helping them identify others.

If the first anxiety signal is behavioral, such as hiding or aggression, the child may be on the impulsive side. Many parents assume that such behavior is purely manipulative. Reframe this behavior to parents as a response to anxiety to promote empathy and a less authoritarian style.

Relaxation

Determine what relaxation strategies are best suited for your child client by asking the parents when they see their child being most calm. While some form of deep breathing is good standard practice, some kids' relaxation response is best engaged via calming music or sounds, pleasant aromas (e.g., essential oils), or soft materials (e.g., a soft blanket or a smooth worry stone). Remind parents of how important it is to model relaxation while they encourage their child to relax, such as breathing along with them and speaking softly, slowly, and warmly.

Although many parents are not thrilled with the amount of technology at a child's disposal, a handy set of earbuds to supply calming music can be very helpful in a pinch. In addition, some children will need to be ushered to a different nearby location to relax if their immediate environment is highly stimulating. Encourage parents to plan for such occurrences whenever possible.

Redirection

Redirection in the form of an action/distraction plan can be helpful, such as assembling a first aid kit that a child preoccupied with potential injury can carry along on a vacation. Still, many children may persist with their worries. Assist parents by preparing them for such persistence and encourage them to be ready to redirect their child with a distraction.

Avoid being overly direct with children about how they should use distraction. The most effective distraction techniques relate to the child's interests and strengths (e.g., a sport, video game, artistic talent, or favorite show or character). Be sure to spend ample time exploring the child's interests so you can better assist them in developing their own unique distraction methods.

Creative Corner

Effective use of the 3 R's requires practice, so why not make it fun? Help the child *recognize* their anxiety by creating their own silly or mischievous (not scary) "anxiety creature." Tap their imagination for how to best *relax* with the power of pretend play. Promote *redirection* by exploring what would happen if their wildest dream came true.

TREATMENT HIGHLIGHTS

- Teach children and parents the 3 R's of anxiety management: recognize, relax, and redirect.

- Help children recognize anxiety by reviewing the psychoeducational information from chapter 2.

- Promote relaxation via mindfulness-based strategies as covered in chapter 5.

- Remember to help children redirect anxious thoughts and behavior into activities that are productive or distracting.

Teaching Kids Effective Self-Expression and Support-Seeking

As previously mentioned, anxious kids don't only cause parental concern; they can provoke intense frustration as well. While some express their anxiety overtly by repeating irrational worries, demanding definitive answers, and persisting with obsessions, others bottle up their distressing thoughts and feelings, resulting in somatic complaints, emotional outbursts, and behavioral issues. No matter how these anxious habits show up, they can leave parents highly irritated in the moment, drained at the end of the day, and feeling more and more guilty over time.

Certainly, anxiety-ridden children need their parents' support. This chapter provides guidelines for helping anxious kids reach out for the support they need *and* for helping parents equip and empower their anxious kids. Teaching kids how to better identify their anxious thoughts and feelings, then communicate them with less emotional intensity, can prevent parent-child conflict and subsequent parental guilt. Also included are activities designed to help anxious kids practice expressing themselves in a healthy manner and seek parental support more effectively.

Helping Anxious Kids Seek Parental Support

In chapter 6, we touched on the fact that repetitive conversations about the content of a kid's anxiety (the specific thoughts and sensations) only serve to strengthen the anxiety. Discussing a child's anxiety through the 3 R's approach will help them recognize their anxiety as a brain issue rather than as being factually credible. The following techniques can help smooth the transition between the child's anxiety showing up and the parent providing the support they need.

Reaching Out

When in session, help the child brainstorm clear statements to use when seeking help from trusted adults, such as "My brain needs some help with worries right now" or "My stomach hurts and I think it's because my brain is working too hard." Inform the parents that you are encouraging their child to communicate when needing support, citing some of the specific statements you have provided.

For at-home practice, I recommend that parents initially model such statements regarding their own concerns or distress—for example, "I'm worrying a lot right now about work. I really need to find a way to relax so I can calm my brain and come up with a plan." The parent can then encourage their child to use similar statements when their child is in an anxious state. Decades of research demonstrates the powerful effects of modeling on children's behavior, and this applies to emotional communication as well.

Role-Playing

Role-playing can also be helpful in teaching children to seek support in ways that do not reinforce the anxiety. Consider role-playing with parents as well so they can reinforce their child's healthy support-seeking.

Reframing

Children's anxiety usually focuses on one or a few themes. These themes can be discerned by paying attention to their questions, worries, and requests for help. Commonplace areas of concern include the following:

- **Safety:** "What if someone shoots up my school?" "I'm afraid that Dad's plane is going to crash."

- **Health:** "What if I have cancer?" "My headache is really bad—what if it never goes away?"

- **Performance:** "I'm going to fail this test!" "I'm afraid I'll mess up and make our team lose the game."

- **Social:** "What if nobody in my class likes me?" "What if I say something stupid in front of my friends?"

- **Global/existential matters:** "What if there's a nuclear war?" "How do I know I'm going to heaven when I die?"

Once you have identified the themes behind the child's anxiety, you can reframe these anxious statements as *values*. For example, in response to the concern about the child's father being in a plane crash, I might say, "Being worried about your dad's safety is your brain's way of saying how much you love him." To the child who is worried about school performance, I might respond, "Your worries about failing the test mean that you care about doing well in school." Then you (or the parent) can move on to helping the child relax their body and finally redirecting them with productive problem-solving or a fun or interesting distraction. (A worksheet to help parents practice reframing is included in chapter 8, p. 89.)

Additional Considerations for Teens

Teens are complex when it comes to seeking parental support. First, the quality of their relationship with their parents largely determines whether or not they will even consider approaching a parent with their distress. If a parent-teen relationship isn't very solid, encouraging the teen to seek support from that parent will be useless, perhaps even detrimental. In such cases, help the teen identify an adult in their life (such as an aunt, uncle, grandparent, teacher, or parent of a close friend) whom they trust. The teen may find it easiest to start by paving the way for a later discussion with the adult:

> "Would it be okay if I talk to you sometimes? I can get pretty anxious and I think you'd understand."

When the parent-teen relationship is reasonably close (which is itself a good treatment goal), be sure you have prepared the parent on how and how not to respond to their teen's anxiety. Since many parents have a pattern of minimizing, dismissing, or reacting angrily to their teen's expression of anxiety, I find it helpful to validate the parent's frustration and then model alternative ways of responding to their teen. I encourage the parent to say something like:

> "I know that's a really tough worry for you to let go of. Let's talk with Dr. O'Brien to see how we can work through these worries."

Explore the various scenarios that the parent encounters with their teen, and then follow up by role-playing with the parent using such alternative phrases.

Once you have a good grasp of the parent-teen dynamics, assist the teen with communication strategies for sharing their feelings with their parent when struggling with anxiety. Be sure to remind the teen that parents can often be very busy and preoccupied; giving their parent a heads-up will increase the odds that the interaction starts off well:

> "Mom, I need to talk with you soon—I'm feeling really anxious. Is now a good time?"

TIPS WITH TEENS

- Teens can have difficulty reaching out to their parents for support for many reasons, such as trust issues, fear of strong emotional reactions, or lack of an adequate bond. Be sure to explore the factors that prevent the teen from reaching out.

- It may take time for the teen to be ready to risk the vulnerability that comes with seeking support from other adults, let alone a parent. Consider role-playing with teens to help them feel more prepared and less anxious about disclosing their emotions or bringing up sensitive topics to a parent.

- As the therapist, you may be one of the few adults (or even the only adult) that a teen is willing to receive support from. Consider being the voice for the teen until they feel ready to begin speaking with their parent directly.

What Do My Feelings Look Like?

Look at the faces below. Each one shows a different feeling that all kids experience. Still, each kid has their own way of expressing that feeling. Draw your own "feeling face" in each empty circle to show what your emotions look like to both you and others.

Happy	Mad
Sad	Worried
Scared	Frustrated
Confused	Excited

Adjusting Your Anxiety Thermostat

Anxiety can be thought of like the temperature of a room. If anxiety is very low, the room feels cool and comfortable. But as anxiety rises, the room starts to warm up until we might feel very hot and uncomfortable. Color in the thermometer below to read your "anxiety temperature." Then, with your therapist, counselor, or parent, brainstorm some things you can do to help lower your anxiety temperature when you start feeling uncomfortable.

Anxiety Thermometer

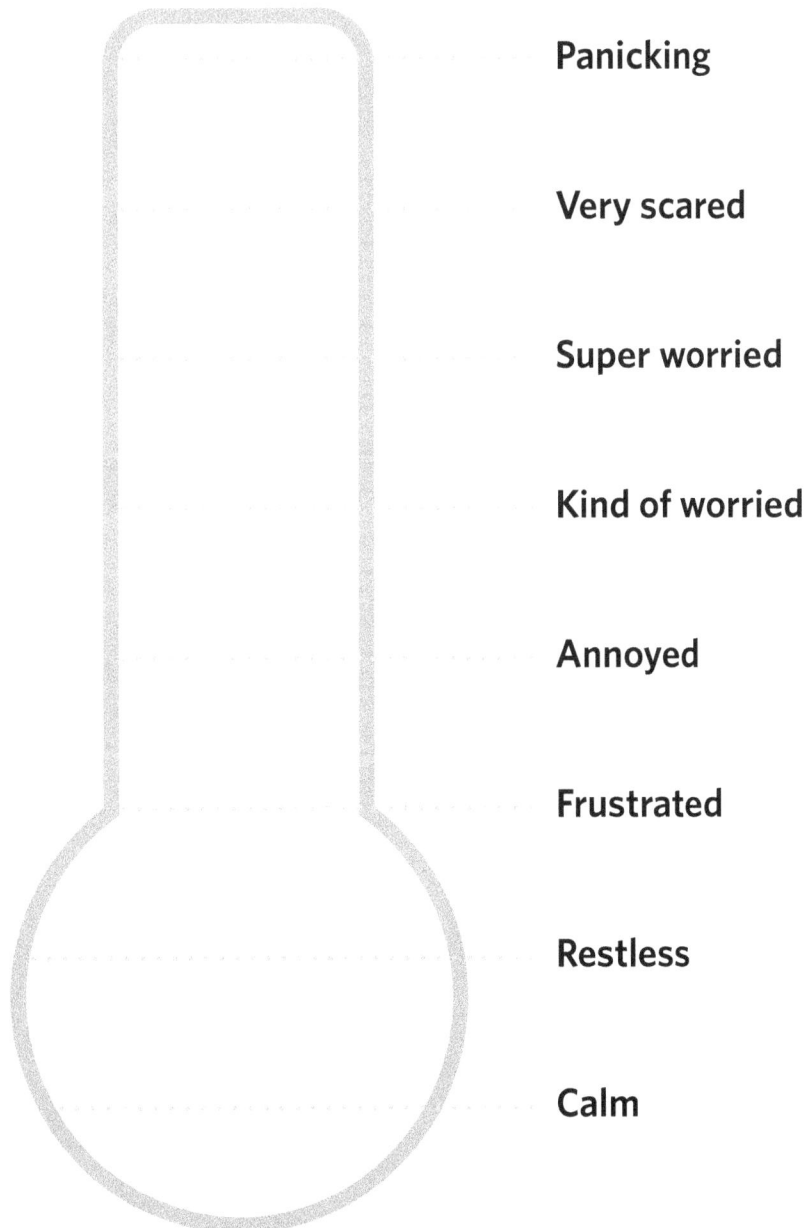

Panicking

Very scared

Super worried

Kind of worried

Annoyed

Frustrated

Restless

Calm

Ways I Can Cool Down

1. When I'm really bored, restless, or fidgety, I can _____

   _____

   _____.

2. When I'm frustrated because something isn't going the way I'd like, I can _____

   _____

   _____.

3. When I get annoyed with someone or with a situation, I can _____

   _____

   _____.

4. Whenever I start becoming nervous or worried, I can _____

   _____

   _____.

5. When I become kind of scared or afraid, I can _____

   _____

   _____.

6. If I become so uncomfortable that I begin to panic, I'll remember _____

   _____

   _____.

How to Ask for Help When I'm Feeling Worried or Scared

It's important to ask adults for help when you aren't able to calm yourself or make yourself feel better. *How you ask can really make a difference in how quickly and easily you get the help you need. When you're able to tell a trusted adult how you're feeling and that you need some help, they can start helping right away!* First, read through the examples below. Then, with your therapist, counselor, or parent, come up with some other ways that you can practice reaching out for help.

What I'm Feeling	What Would Help Me	What I Can Say to Ask for Help
I'm feeling really worried and my stomach hurts.	I want my dad to help me figure out how I can calm my brain and body.	"Dad, my stomach hurts and I think it's because my brain is working too hard. Can you help me?"
I'm so nervous about my math test tomorrow that I can't focus on studying.	I need help relaxing so I can finish studying and then get plenty of rest tonight.	"Mom, I'm worrying a lot right now about my math test. Can you help me find a way to relax and prepare well?"

What I'm Feeling	What Would Help Me	What I Can Say to Ask for Help

TREATMENT HIGHLIGHTS

- Determine the child's typical way of expressing anxiety to their parents.

- Assess parent-child interactions that may promote frustration or guilt on the part of parents and kids.

- Begin changing negative parent-child communication patterns by first identifying the child's anxiety themes.

- Reframe the child's worries as values and brainstorm healthier statements for expression and support-seeking.

- Role play alternative interchanges with both kids and parents.

CHAPTER 8

Connecting With Kids Without Asking "What's Wrong?"

Well-intentioned parents often ask distressed kids questions like "What's wrong?" "Are you okay?" "How are you feeling?"

You can guess the usual responses: "Nothing." "I'm fine." "Good."

These well-intentioned inquiries usually result in either avoidance or conflict: "Why won't you talk to me? I can't help you if you don't tell me what's wrong!"

Anxious children are often torn between wanting to open up for relief and wanting to stay closed off to avoid the very anxiety they are experiencing. While it's vital to connect with the distress of anxious kids, *how* parents speak is just as important, if not more so, than what is said.

A more useful way for parents to tune in to their child's needs and encourage meaningful dialogue is to model appropriate *self-disclosure*. To teach this skill, I encourage parents to think about some of their daily thoughts and feelings that may be distressing, worrisome, or confusing. Parents can then look for opportunities to share some of their inner dialogue (Jiang et al., 2017).

To ensure this sharing is helpful, I suggest parents avoid extremes in what and how they share. One extreme would be revealing highly detailed, sensitive, and unnecessary information that would place the child into the world of adult concerns; understandably, this is likely to make the child even more anxious. The other extreme is telling the child "everything is okay" when it is obvious to the child that something is wrong. While this might seem harmless, it can also evoke additional anxiety, since just the parent's facial expression or tone can cause an anxious kid to imagine a worst-case scenario.

The most beneficial disclosures for children highlight an authentic thought or feeling in a general but relatable manner and end on a positive note:

> "Today was stressful at work. People were angry about some new rules and it was uncomfortable. But I'm going to take some time tonight to think about what I can do to have a better day tomorrow. Plus, I can talk to one of my friends for some ideas."

This middle-ground kind of disclosure—honest without being unnecessarily detailed—not only models emotional expression, but also implies that support from others is healthy and helpful.

Timing Is Everything

Have you ever arrived home after a long day of work, only to be immediately bombarded with questions by a well-intentioned loved one? Even adults tend to find this overwhelming, and children, especially those struggling with anxiety, feel even more overwhelmed by such questioning during a transition, such as from school to home. Parents can reduce their child's transitional anxiety by limiting their questions to those that may serve the child's needs—for example, asking whether the child is hungry, thirsty, or tired. I encourage inquisitive parents to hold off on questions about the child's previous environment (e.g., school or their other parent's home) until the child has settled in. Although it depends on the individual child, young children often need 20 to 30 minutes, and preteens and teens even more time, to adjust and decompress. In fact, I often hear parents say that they learn more about their child's day later in the afternoon or evening.

Accessing Thoughts and Feelings in Anxious Kids

Like parents, therapists must also be mindful of how they ask an anxious child about their thoughts and feelings. Well-intentioned therapists may move too quickly when seeking to promote self-expression, especially around sensitive topics. Remember that while you are quite accustomed to your therapeutic setting, this is new and unfamiliar ground for the child. By following the steps below, you can gradually promote self-expression in anxious children.

1. As mentioned in chapter 1, asking children about their interests is an effective method for initiating self-disclosure. Start by reapproaching the interests they shared from a more cognitive and emotional angle:

    "Tell me what you think is most fun about playing Roblox."

    "How do you feel when you are doing well at the game?"

    "What sometimes gets frustrating about it? What do you think or feel when the game gets difficult?"

2. Once the child has expressed themselves both cognitively and emotionally about their interests, you can ask similar thought-feeling questions about school and eventually about their family. Remember to approach less sensitive topics first and focus more on their thoughts before easing into questions about their feelings. By doing so, you're beginning with less threatening material and gradually increasing the level of challenge.

3. Another useful approach is the Five Feelings exercise. This technique involves asking the child about what situations tend to make them feel a certain way.

    • Starting with a basic feeling like happy, mad, sad, worried, or scared, ask the child about a situation that evokes this feeling: "What is something that makes you feel happy?" or "When do you usually feel happy?"

- Continue with three additional feelings. I recommend proceeding from positive feelings to more vulnerable emotional experiences. Depending on the child's responsiveness and developmental level, consider adding one or two more complex feelings, such as loneliness or disappointment, or any feelings you believe are relevant to the child's situation.

- End the exercise by asking about a positive feeling that's easy for the child to share about, such as, "When do you feel the most excited?"

- Depending on the child's age, consider going through the Five Feelings exercise twice. The first time, ask what situations or *external* events relate to the feelings: "When is a time you feel ___?" The second time, relate your questions to their *internal* experiences: "What's a thought that makes you feel ___?" Remember to begin and end emotional conversations with more positive feeling states. The middle of the conversation can be more sensitive in nature.

An overarching guideline when speaking with children in session about thoughts and feelings is to follow the "thermostat rule." That is, sessions should generally begin with "cool" (casual, easy-to-discuss) material, then gradually move on to "warmer" (more sensitive) material, before briefly touching on a "hot" (highly sensitive) topic with caution and discretion. As the session progresses, be sure to lower the emotional temperature by returning to less heated topics, and always end on a cool and comfortable note.

Alternatively, you can keep the emotional temperature of the room well regulated by addressing two or three sensitive topics followed by one or two lighter topics throughout the session. Regardless, *always avoid* ending a session on serious or sensitive emotional materials. This method is a good idea for parent sessions as well!

Helping Parents Connect With Their Anxious, Resistant Teen

Anxious, resistant teens often present as guarded, shut down, irritable, and even verbally explosive at times. None of these characteristics make it easy for parents to connect. In fact, adolescents who express anxiety through defensiveness or aggression may alienate themselves from much-needed parental support.

It's important to help parents recognize that they can't soothe their anxious, resistant teen unless the teen senses the parent is in a calm state and thus safe to approach. With this in mind, I sometimes encourage parents to think of their teen as a temperamental cat in distress: "Your 'cat' needs comforting, but when you approach them, the cat either flees, hisses, or scratches you. How fun is that?!" This metaphor helps parents see the value of self-regulating and remaining patient until their "temperamental cat" comes to them.

Unfortunately, the "cat" may often approach the parents at inconvenient times (e.g., late at night or in the middle of household tasks). However, these are the times when teens are most receptive to connection. Assist parents with the following step-by-step approach for connecting with their anxious, resistant teen.

- First, express **appreciation**: "I'm really glad you're telling me about this."

  Doing this immediately upon being approached conveys nonjudgmental acceptance, which will immediately begin to reduce the teen's anxiety.

  Note: It's better for one rather than two parents to be involved in this moment to reduce the chances of the teen feeling bombarded.

- Next, **reflect and validate** the teen: "It sounds like you're saying ___. It's understandable to feel/think that way; many people would feel the same."

  Reflection ensures that the parent is reading the teen accurately, while validation helps the teen feel heard, understood, and less alone in their perception.

  Note: Inform parents that accurate reflection is necessary before validation. I tell parents that the best sign of an accurate reflection is when the teen responds with "Yes, exactly!" If their teen's response is the classic, "You don't understand!" they'll need to ask their teen to retell their concerns so the parent can truly understand. Teach parents to pay just as much attention to their teen's emotional state as they do to the content of the message. Over time, assist the parents with reflecting both thoughts and emotions, which will help their teen feel more understood.

- Third, show **empathy**: "I bet that isn't easy" or "That's probably pretty upsetting."

  This expresses genuine care and concern in a more powerful way than just saying "I understand."

- Finally, invite **collaboration**: "Maybe we can come up with a way to manage this. If you have any ideas or want to hear some of mine, let me know."

  Caution parents against rushing to a potential solution, as their teen may not be ready to hear or act upon it. A gradual, collaborative approach to finding solutions is likely to be more effective.

  Recognize that some teens just need to be heard. They may either reapproach the parent later for input or come up with their own way to address the situation. I encourage parents to ask, "Do you need me to listen or do you need help coming up with some ideas for a solution?"

Identifying the Values Fueling Your Child's Worries

Anxiety-ridden kids tend to be highly conscientious. They often approach their parents with "What if..." or "I'm really scared that..." statements. Identifying the values associated with your child's anxiety can help you respond in a more effective manner.

Here are some of the common themes of kids' worries:

Safety

- "What if someone breaks into our house and hurts us?"
- "What if someone shoots up my school?"
- "What if I can't find you at the store and someone takes me?"
- "What are we going to do if a tornado or hurricane destroys our house?"
- "I'm scared that you're going to die in a car accident."

Health

- "What if I get sick?"
- "My headache is really bad—what if it never goes away?"
- "What if I have cancer?"
- "I'm scared that you're going to have a heart attack."
- "I can't do gymnastics—I'm going to fall and hit my head!"

Performance

- "I'm going to fail this test!"
- "What if I forget to do my homework?"
- "I'm afraid I'll mess up and make our team lose the game."
- "What if I forget my lines in the play?"
- "What if I get in trouble at school?"

Social

- "What if I say something stupid in front of my friends?"
- "What if nobody in my class likes me?"

- "What if no one wants to hang out with me?"
- "What if kids are mean to me?"
- "I'm worried that I won't have anyone to sit with at lunch."

Global/Existential Matters

- "What will we do if there's a nuclear war?"
- "What will happen to me if you die?"
- "What if pollution destroys the planet?"
- "How do I know I'm going to heaven when I die?"
- "Why does anything matter if we're all going to die?"

Once you've identified the theme behind your child's anxious statement, you can reframe it to reflect your child's values. Doing so can be a very effective way to reduce their anxiety. For example, if your child says, "I'm afraid that Dad's plane is going to crash," you might respond, "Being worried about Dad's safety is your brain's way of saying how much you love him." Or if they express concern about failing a test, you might say, "Your worries about failing the test mean that you care about doing well in school."

Give it a try: First, write down a few of your child's worries—either the most common statements they make or those they've shared most recently. Next, identify the values behind these worries. Finally, think of how you can respond to your child when they approach you with these worries, making sure to reframe them in terms of your child's values.

My Child's Worry	My Child's Values	My Response

Approaching Your Distressed Child

As a parent, you often sense when your child is in distress. With the intention of being helpful, it's common to ask questions like "What's wrong?" or "Is everything okay?" Unfortunately, such questions often result in answers like "Nothing" or "Everything is fine." Consider some of the following strategies for approaching your distressed child:

- Be mindful of timing. Postpone any intervention if your child is:

  » Engrossed in an activity

  » In the middle of a transition (e.g., coming home or leaving for school)

  » Seeking time alone

- Observe and comment before questioning.

  » "It looks like you're thinking about something."

  » "I notice you're looking . . ." (e.g., confused, worried, frustrated)

  » "Seems like you're moving really fast/slow today."

- Offer an invitation to share.

  » "I'll touch base with you later."

  » "Well remember, I love you."

  » "I'm going to fold the laundry and could use your company."

Child-Friendly Tips for Emotional Conversations

"How are you feeling about . . . ?" or "What do you think about . . . ?" are common ways to encourage emotional expression in children. However, open-ended questions are often overwhelming for distressed kids. Instead, consider the more structured approaches below.

Multiple Choice Method

- "Many kids feel frustrated, annoyed, or angry in a situation like this. What about you?"

- "I wonder if you're feeling more disappointed, down, or just don't care much about this?"

- "I might feel hopeless, sad, or lonely about this, but I'm not sure what you feel about it."

Fill In the Blank

- "Kids can have lots of thoughts or feelings about this situation. How would you finish this sentence? 'When it comes to school I just ___.'"

- "Many people wish things were different sometimes. Could you finish this sentence? 'If I could change one thing, I would ___.'"

- "How would you finish this sentence? 'It seems like I'm almost always thinking or feeling ___.'"

Color Systems

- "If red is angry, orange is annoyed, and yellow is frustrated, what color would you choose to show how you feel right now?"

- "What color would you choose to show how you feel about your brother/sister right now?"

- "What color do you want to feel less and what color do you want to feel more?"

- "What is something that makes your color really red?"

Rating Scales

- "If 0 is feeling good and 5 is really angry, what's your number right now?"

- "You said you're worried about your math test. If 1 is a little worried, 5 is pretty worried, and 10 is super worried, what number are you?"

- "You said that your anger is an 8. What's something that we could do to lower the number?"

TREATMENT HIGHLIGHTS

- Provide parents with alternatives for asking kids about thoughts and feelings beyond "What's wrong?"

- Teach parents "middle-ground" self-disclosure to model emotional transparency, optimism, and problem-solving.

- Ask children about their interests from a cognitive-emotional perspective.

- Consider the Five Feelings exercise and the "emotional thermostat" method for promoting self-expression.

CHAPTER 9

Fight, Flight, and Freeze: Combating Panic and Phobias

Anxiety is a powerful force that can create strong reactions. Even though many clients are familiar with the fight, flight, and freeze responses to anxiety, these intense effects can frighten and alarm children (and sometimes their parents too). However, when kids and parents understand why these reactions occur, fear dissipates, and empowerment begins to develop.

Panic in particular can be challenging to recognize in young children. Tantrums, zoned-out looks, and abrupt aggressive behavior can all be expressions of panic. Childhood phobias often accompany panic and sometimes serve as precursors to panic episodes. For example, a child with a needle phobia who hears that it's time to go to the doctor may suddenly become panic-stricken. Phobias can strengthen panic and panic can reinforce phobias, leading to a vicious anxiety cycle.

Part of our work as therapists is assisting parents to better identify and understand the contributors to panic episodes. It's equally critical that we teach parents to co-regulate, as children can regulate their emotions better around well-regulated adults.

This chapter focuses on helping families identify, understand, prepare for, and cope with the fight, flight, and freeze responses associated with panic disorder. Guidelines for how to address phobias with systematic desensitization in a youth-friendly manner are also provided.

Identifying Manifestations of Panic

Keep in mind that panic may take physiological, cognitive, and behavioral forms. Children and teens vary as to which types of symptoms are most dominant and impairing.

Physiological Symptoms

- Racing heartbeat
- Rapid/shallow breathing
- Hyperventilation
- Holding breath or difficulty breathing

- Throat tightening/difficulty swallowing

- Flushed face

- Feeling hot/sweaty

- Uncomfortable skin sensations (e.g., "bugs crawling on skin")

- Chest pains

- Nausea

- Pit or "butterflies" in stomach

- Headache

Cognitive Symptoms

- Intense worry about health

- Fear of dying (self or others)

- Catastrophic/fatalistic thinking

- Extreme black-and-white/absolute thinking

Behavioral Symptoms

- Extreme avoidance of perceived threats

- High agitation

- Oppositional/defiant behavior

- Tantrums

- Intense tearfulness and whining

- Uncontrollable sobbing

- Screaming/yelling

- Physical aggression or destruction

Understanding Panic

When panic takes over, your body can feel uncomfortable, your thoughts can be scary, and your behavior might feel out of your control. Learn more about how your brain and body show panic by putting a check mark next to any of the items below that you think, feel, or notice when you are in a state of panic.

My Body Feels . . .

☐ Warm or even hot

☐ Sweaty or sticky

☐ Tingly or itchy

☐ Hurt in my head

☐ Hurt in my stomach

☐ Like I'm going to be sick/throw up

My Thoughts Can Be . . .

☐ Worries about my health

☐ Fears of dying

☐ Afraid I'll never see someone again

☐ That something very bad is going to happen

☐ That I am not safe

My Behavior Might Look Like . . .

☐ Running away or hiding

☐ Hitting or fighting

☐ Throwing or breaking something

☐ Shouting, "No!"

☐ Lots of crying or whining

☐ Screaming or yelling

How My Child's Panic Shows Itself

Panic can take many forms depending on your child's age, temperament, family history, and experiences. Panic can often be confusing and scary for both you and your child. Complete the following statements to determine your child's unique expression of panic.

When My Child Is in a Panic State, They . . .

1. Complain most about _____

   _____

   _____

   _____.

2. Express intense fears about _____

   _____

   _____

   _____.

3. Feel especially_____

   _____

   _____

   _____.

4. Show problem behaviors like _____

   _____

   _____

   _____.

Preparing for Panic

When panic happens, kids feel scared, confused, and out of control. Sometimes they even think they are very sick or are going to die. But remember, panic doesn't mean that something terrible is definitely going to happen; all it means for sure is that there are too many anxiety chemicals moving around in your brain. Being prepared can really help you feel less scared and more in control. Fill in the thought bubbles below to help you be better prepared for panic.

The last time I felt super-scary anxiety, I thought:

The next time I start to feel super-scary anxiety, I will:

Discovering My Child's Preferred Soothing Style

While slow, deep breathing tends to help calm many kids, children often require other ways to begin feeling calmer. Learn more about your child's preferred ways of soothing by jotting down what comes to mind under the following headings.

1. Sounds that soothe my child include: _____

    _____

    _____

    _____

2. Images that soothe my child include: _____

    _____

    _____

    _____

3. Materials or textures that soothe my child include: _____

    _____

    _____

    _____

4. Activities that soothe my child include: _____

    _____

    _____

    _____

Creating a Desensitization "Challenge Ladder" for Kids' Fears and Phobias

You are likely familiar with the technique of systematic desensitization, also called graduated exposure therapy. This evidence-based approach combines relaxation techniques with gradual exposure to anxiety-producing stimuli. While the technique has strong scientific support, it is often minimally effective with children *unless* it is adequately modified in child-friendly, developmentally appropriate ways. To address this obstacle, I find a "challenge ladder" to be a useful method for kids. Here are the basic steps in developing and using a challenge ladder to address a child's fears:

1. Explore the child's fears and phobias. If there are several, determine which one to address first. It is often best to begin with the phobia that is most impairing or the one that the child is most receptive to working on.

2. Gently discuss the most anxiety-producing stimuli or situations for the child and inform them, "We will start with something much less scary than that."

3. Assess the least anxiety-producing stimuli (imagined/visualized, illustrated, photographic, or in real life) through a collaborative discussion. Help the child identify increasingly less threatening situations until you find a mildly anxiety-producing scenario to begin with.

4. Allow the child to label the first "rung" of the ladder with their first challenge. For example, if the child has a fear of dogs, they might decide that their first challenge will be to imagine standing near a big dog on leash. Invite them to use words, drawings, stickers, and so forth to denote the challenge. Some children may enjoy drawing their own challenge ladder, possibly with your assistance. Encourage creativity in the ladder's design.

5. Encourage the child to think of other challenges to note as they make progress; add these to the ladder accordingly.

6. Ask the child to name supportive adults—such as parents, older siblings, or extended family—who can help them practice slowly going up the ladder.

7. Review anxiety-management skills like deep breathing, mindfulness, and redirection. (Review chapters 3 through 6 for more.)

8. Inform and engage the parent about the challenge ladder in separate parent meetings. Be sure to provide guidelines for repeated practice at home and encourage a repetitive schedule for practice. Encourage the parent to move slowly up the ladder to facilitate the child's success and confidence. Finally, prepare the parent for regression and instruct them to revisit the previous rung on the ladder if the child is not ready to move forward.

9. Assist children and parents in modifying challenges to promote greater success. For example, some ladders may need more low-level challenges or other changes to ensure that the progression from one level of anxiety to the next moves at a realistic pace for the child.

10. Evaluate progress and areas of difficulty with both the parent and child. Use your judgment and collaborate with the child to determine whether these discussions are best conducted in joint or separate parent/child sessions.

Creative Corner

Tap into a child's tech savvy by mutually exploring the latest apps, videos, and virtual reality devices to enhance their challenge ladder. For example, you might invite a child who is phobic of thunderstorms to assist you in a YouTube search in order to find and rank thunderstorm videos from least to most anxiety producing. By integrating technology with desensitization, you'll increase the chances of the child practicing these scenarios and thus reducing their fears about them.

Creating My Challenge Ladder

Facing fears takes work, but just like climbing a ladder, each step brings you closer to your goal. Use the challenge ladder below to keep track of your progress in dealing with your fears. Be sure to give yourself credit every time you practice, especially when you're ready for the next step. How far up the ladder do you think you can go?

Helping Your Child Overcome Fear With Their Challenge Ladder

Childhood fears and phobias can seem insurmountable. However, progress can be made when parents, therapists, and kids work as a team. Consider the following method for overcoming childhood fears, called the **challenge ladder** approach. Meet with your child's therapist as needed for additional support and assistance.

1. With their therapist's help, your child will create a challenge ladder of exposure to their feared situation or issue. They will identify a manageable challenge to start with, followed by a series of increasingly difficult challenges leading up to your child's ultimate goal. (For example, if your child has a fear of dogs, they might choose watching a video of puppies as their first challenge and work their way up to petting a friendly dog in real life.)

2. Schedule specific days and times to help your child practice exposure to their feared situation or issue. Provide your child with options regarding the timing of the exposure experiences, and allow your child to select supportive people (besides yourself) to help them with some of the exposure practices.

3. Help your child move slowly—not quickly—up the ladder to facilitate their success and confidence. After your child has completed one challenge, ask them to begin working on the next rung of the ladder during your next practice. If your child's anxiety and resistance get in the way, reduce the challenge with input from your child, but do not enable complete avoidance. They may choose to repeat their most recently completed challenge if they are not ready to move forward, but they should not skip practicing altogether.

4. Discuss and provide rewarding experiences for any significant progress your child makes.

TREATMENT HIGHLIGHTS

- Help parents understand how their child's anxiety manifests. Does their panicked child tend to be verbally or physically aggressive (fight), avoid or flee the situation (flight), or zone out in confusion (freeze)?

- Assist parents in determining the most effective methods for soothing their panicked child.

- Use systematic desensitization to address fears and phobias through use of a "challenge ladder."

- Collaborate with the parents and child to develop and modify the ladder and reevaluate the child's progress. Assist with any additional modifications as needed.

CHAPTER 10

Attached at the Hip: Action Plans for Separation Anxiety Disorder

While separation anxiety is developmentally common in young children, especially as they enter the preschool years, some children experience intense and debilitating separation anxiety even after months of repeated separations and reunions with their parents. The parents may become highly concerned about their child's ability to function without their presence. In fact, they are often concerned that their child is being "traumatized" by the separation. I remind these parents that distress does not equal trauma. While children may be distressed, they can learn to tolerate and eventually cope with the separation if the parents change their typical responses.

Highly distressed parents, who themselves may suffer from anxiety, often unintentionally enable and strengthen their child's separation distress. Excessive reassurance, lengthy explanations, and elongated departures only serve to exacerbate the anxiety. Keep in mind that parents of children with separation anxiety are often preoccupied with their child's safety and may experience acute distress and guilt in response to their child's discomfort. Therefore, helping parents better regulate their distress and self-soothe is a key component of separation anxiety treatment.

Experience has taught me that many kids with separation anxiety aren't just worried about being apart from their caretakers, but may in fact be consumed with fears about their own and their parents' safety, security, and well-being when they are apart. It is common for these youngsters to imagine horrible tragedies befalling themselves or their families while separated: "What if my mom gets into a car accident?" "What if I get really sick and need Dad to take me to the hospital?" Assessing for other types of anxiety is necessary for these kids, since separation anxiety often goes hand-in-hand with a specific phobia, generalized anxiety disorder, or panic disorder. If so, effective treatment will need to address these areas as well.

This chapter will offer strategies for treating children with separation anxiety, guidance in developing action plans for managing separation anxiety in different settings, and tools for empowering both kids and parents to cope with the distress associated with being apart.

First Things First: Assisting Parents With Self-Regulation

Children with separation anxiety often come by it honestly. Besides the likelihood of a significant family history of anxiety, many of these kids share a slow-to-warm up temperament with one of their parents. A mom with an anxiety-prone disposition may identify strongly with her child's anxiety and feel considerable empathy for the child. However, strong empathy can lead to feeling as distressed as the child. It then follows that the child's distress may be very intolerable for the parent, making them desperate to relieve the child's anxiety as quickly as possible. Providing immediate relief, although well-intentioned, interferes with the child's ability to develop self-soothing strategies.

One of the first steps in treating kids with separation anxiety is to assist the parents in recognizing how their own distress can complicate their child's tolerance of separation. Being nonjudgmental is extremely important in this endeavor; I find it helpful to frequently empathize with the parent's own feelings of anxiety, guilt, and exasperation.

I also help parents make a distinction between distress and trauma by providing the perspective that some level of distress is necessary for growth. Specifically, distress due to separation is necessary because it provides children with opportunities to develop better emotional regulation. By the same token, it is critical to teach the parents skills for managing their own distress *before* treating the child's separation anxiety. Encourage parents to regularly practice mindfulness and other relaxation strategies to reduce the intensity of their distress reactions. (Refer to chapters 5 and 6 for some ideas.)

The Initial Session With Children Experiencing Separation Anxiety

The initial therapy session with a child who struggles with separation anxiety can be quite challenging, particularly in the moment before the parent leaves the therapy office. Preparing the parent beforehand (during the initial parent interview) is necessary so that they know their role in the session. When parents feel confident and secure about therapy from the onset, you're setting the stage for effective separation anxiety treatment.

1. Conduct a parent-only initial interview (or two) with a focus on parental self-regulation. Use this to set guidelines for your first session with the child, including how you will manage possible separation anxiety in the first session.

2. Assure the parent that *you* will be responsible for managing the child's distress in the session, rather than the parent.

3. Instruct the parent to make only one statement that instills faith in the child's ability to cope:

   "I know you are scared, but Dr. O'Brien will help you feel more comfortable soon."

4. Encourage the parent to bring something to read (or provide them with a questionnaire) for the first session. Doing so allows the focus to be on you and the child, rather than on the parent-child relationship.

5. If the child seeks parental reassurance, instruct the parent to repeat the empowering statement from step 3. Again, the parent should be minimally responsive to the child so the focus remains on the child-therapist interaction.

6. When possible, provide the child with options for exploring the room and engaging with materials. Offer to participate in play or a game, but do not attempt to persuade the child. Rather, accept the child's level of adjustment and occasionally provide reflection and validation:

   "It seems like you're not quite ready for Mom to leave the room, and that's okay. Sometimes kids need more time to feel comfortable."

7. Keep your statements focused on the play and art materials rather than on the child:

   "I see that you found the dollhouse. The furniture and family figures are in the basket next to it."

8. Use your clinical judgment as to whether or when to ask the parent to leave the room. Instruct the parent beforehand to simply state that they will be in the waiting room. Inform the child that they may ask to see their parent at any time, and that you will walk them back to their parent after the session ends. If the child cannot tolerate the separation, the parent can remain in the room, but they should resume reading or completing a form rather than focusing on the child.

"Feel-Better Kits" for Easing Separation Anxiety

A primary difficulty for children with separation anxiety is leaving the comfort and familiarity associated with their parent or household and transitioning to a less familiar and less predictable environment. However, separation distress can occur even when a child is very familiar with their upcoming surroundings. Parents are often confused as to why such familiarity doesn't provide more comfort.

Remind parents that anxiety isn't rational and that their child's separation distress has more to do with feeling overwhelmed by physical sensations (e.g., tight chest, stomach pain) or by racing worries about catastrophic events.

Providing children with materials for self-soothing and healthy distraction can ease their transition from one environment to another. I encourage kids and parents to create "feel-better kits" that they can bring along to the next environment and keep with them upon separation. Such kits can include worry stones, a small stuffed animal, pocket-sized games or puzzles, and even child-friendly aromatherapy items. Feel-better kits are most effective when they are tailored to the ways that the child is most easily soothed and distracted. (See chapter 6 for ways to gather information that will help you to individualize a child's kit.)

Creative Corner

Use a child's natural curiosity to help redirect them from their preoccupation with separation. You might pose questions for them to ponder, such as "I wonder how tall of a tower we can make with these blocks?" or "What do you think your teacher has planned for your class holiday party next week?"

Tips for Preparing Your Anxious Child for Separation

These steps will help you prepare your child to go to school. They can also be modified for other situations.

1. Request assistance *in advance* from a member of the school staff who has a strong rapport with your child. Ask if they can provide additional choices for how your child can begin their day. A fun, low-stress activity can ease the transition to the classroom.

2. Briefly validate your child's fear: "I know it feels scary when you're away from me."

3. Identify the specific person who will reunite with your child and give a relatable time frame: "Grandma will be at the pickup area when the school day is over."

4. If possible, encourage your child to think about an activity they would like to do (or some other type of decision they can make) once the caretaker returns: "You can pick which game you'd like to play with Grandma first, and let her know when you see her."

Getting Ready to Say Goodbye to People I Love

Saying goodbye to people we love can make us feel sad or scared. For example, your brain might tell you that you might not see your loved one again. That's really your brain's way of telling you how much you love that person! Fill in the following sentences to help your brain become less scared about saying goodbye.

1. The hardest or scariest part of leaving my _____

   is _____.

2. When I'm scared to leave my _____, I can

   think about how _____

   will help me feel less scared.

3. When I don't want to go somewhere without _____,

   remembering _____

   can help me feel better.

4. Something I can take with me to feel less worried is _____.

5. Even though it's hard to leave _____, I will

   feel better when I see _____.

TREATMENT HIGHLIGHTS

- Develop a procedure for managing the child's separation anxiety and inform the parent of their role, which includes learning to self-regulate their own anxiety.

- Assess for any co-occurring or underlying contributors or disorders to the child's separation anxiety.

- Assist parents and other involved caretakers in developing a team-approach plan for separation in specific situations (e.g., school, evenings with a babysitter).

- Teach anxious children techniques for self-soothing.

- Advise and assist adults in learning to co-regulate.

- Encourage the use of feel-better kits and transitional objects to ease the separation process for kids.

CHAPTER 11

"But What If . . .?": Treating Generalized Anxiety Disorder

Unfortunately, there are many things in today's world to worry about, and checking the news only reinforces such worry. From natural disasters to global pandemics to mass shootings, our world can feel very unpredictable, unsafe, and out of our control.

Research tells us that anxious kids tend to be highly intelligent and overthink . . . a lot (Gerlach & Gloster, 2020). In other words, these kids often use their considerable intellectual muscle to ruminate on irrational worries until fear overpowers them, leaving them feeling fearful and vulnerable to both everyday stressors and the possibility of catastrophic events. Parents who try to reassure or reason with worried kids soon find they have entered a never-ending cycle that often leaves them at their wit's end: "There's just no way to make them stop worrying—nothing I say helps!"

Even for adults, worry can be debilitating. When well-intentioned friends tell us not to worry, we often feel misunderstood, unsupported, and even more worried. It should be no surprise that children feel similarly; moreover, children often lack realistic perspective, which further fuels their anxiety.

This chapter offers strategies for assisting kids with excessive worry, clinically referred to as generalized anxiety disorder (GAD). It's worth repeating yet again that, while validating a child's feelings is important, excessive or repeated discussion about the *content* of the worry may inadvertently strengthen their anxiety. Instead, the strategies in this chapter will help you empower children to manage worry so it no longer limits their quality of life.

Also, since prolonged anxiety can lead to depression, some children with a long-term history of worry may unknowingly struggle with some level of depression. Such depression can be tricky to recognize, especially if it takes the form of frequent irritability, agitation, negativity, or apathy. Be mindful that these kids may be seen by their parents as excessively negative and unappreciative. These characteristics may be associated with an underlying persistent depressive disorder (also called atypical depression, and formerly known as dysthymic disorder). These kids need treatment for both anxiety and depression. Although depression may improve to a degree as anxiety lessens, be sure to monitor the child's mood over time by both observation and parental report.

Strategies for Assisting Children Who Worry

When approached by a worried child, parents often resort to reassurance. While this seems natural, it is largely ineffective. Anxious children whose brains are in overdrive require more than reassurance to extinguish their fiery thoughts. They need an age-appropriate explanation of what anxiety actually means and how it affects their brain and body. A good place to begin is with a tour of the brain (as discussed in chapter 2, p. 31). Explain how worries come from brain chemicals and encourage children to use a lighthearted label for discrediting the worry, such as "That's the annoying 'what-if voice,' and I'm telling it to chill out." This helps to create some distance between their brain activity and their sense of self, which may promote feelings of safety and security.

The next component for assisting worried kids centers on decreasing their central nervous system activity. Empower children by linking relaxation directly to reducing the worry chemicals. This can be accomplished through the use of relaxation and mindfulness strategies (see chapters 5 and 6). Remember, teaching these techniques will have little impact without adequate practice; it is essential to build in such practice by scheduling "chill time" (much like scheduling workouts).

In addition, relaxation strategies cannot fully combat a climate of chronic stress and tension in a child's home or school environment. Review chapter 4 to determine practical interventions for lowering the "temperature" and slowing the pace. Otherwise, returning to overwhelming environments will only keep a child's brain in overdrive.

Adults, including mental health professionals, often wonder about the origin of children's worries. Some may seem obvious, such as a child who sees or hears about a dog attack or one who experiences sudden physical illness. However, many worries seem quite irrational, such as a kid who worries about aggressive dogs despite having no previous experience with them. Similarly, both parents and clinicians can be at a loss as to why an exceptional student worries about failing.

My experience has taught me that children often worry most about the things they truly value. I find reframing children's worries as values (as discussed in chapters 7 and 8) is very effective for neutralizing some of their anxious energy. Reframing offers them a new perspective while commending them for their strong values and conscientiousness. For example, you might say, "Worrying about your family's safety is your brain's way of telling you how much you love them."

> Be sure to review this concept with parents so they can use this reframing approach as well; you can use the Identifying the Values Fueling Your Child's Worries worksheet from chapter 8 (p. 89).

Still, despite our best efforts, some anxious children do not take easily to learning and practicing relaxation and self-soothing. When you hit therapeutic plateaus with such children, consider helping them convert their worries into productive activity or distraction. Kids with limited ability to relax may need to learn more about how to use healthy redirection. Help them think of other ways they can get their brain or body busy, such as "I think I need to ride my bike now" or "Maybe Mom needs some help with chores." (Review chapter 6 for more redirection guidelines.)

Keep in mind that younger children, especially those under 8 years of age, may respond better to cognitive interventions that integrate creative approaches, such as play therapy. Cognitive-behavioral play therapy methods may include the use of puppets for modeling effective self-talk. For example, a puppet can say, "I'm worried about getting sick because I really like being healthy." There are many good texts available on cognitive-behavioral play therapy that can stimulate your creativity in treating younger worried children (Meersand & Gilmore, 2018; Kaduson & Schaefer, 2021).

Creative Corner

Enhance cognitive techniques like thought-stopping by incorporating kids' favorite video games into the mix. For example, kids can "knock annoying worry zombies" out of their brains just like they do when playing games like Minecraft or Roblox.

Understanding and Responding to My Child's Worries

Well-intentioned parents often try to reassure their worried children, but reassurance is rarely effective with anxious kids. Complete the following sentences to learn more about your child's worries so you can respond more effectively.

1. When my child is worried, they usually say _____

   _____.

2. On a scale of 1 to 10, with 10 being extremely distressed, I would rate my child's distress level

   when worried as _____.

3. I've noticed that my child's worries often have to do with _____

   _____.

4. I usually respond to my child's worries by _____

   _____.

5. My child's reaction to my response is often _____

   _____.

6. Three new ways I can respond to or reframe my child's worry include: _____

   _____

   _____

   _____.

What Do My Worries Really Mean?

Worries can make us feel very uncomfortable, especially when we think bad things are really going to happen. But worries are actually your brain's way of telling you what you really value. Your parent, your therapist, or another adult who knows you well can help you discover the things in life that matter most to you. With their help, fill in the following sentences to learn what your worries really mean.

1. My worries about _____

   actually mean _____

   _____.

2. Whenever I worry about _____,

   I can remember that _____

   is very important to me.

3. Worries that are scary, like _____,

   really mean that _____

   _____.

4. When I can't stop worrying about _____,

   I will try to remember that those worries are really about _____

   _____.

Tips for Helping Your Child With Worry

Sometimes your child will catch you off-guard with an unexpected worry. Other times, you'll hear the same worry over and over again. Below are some tips for responding to your child in these moments, regardless of the kind of worries they may throw your way.

1. **VALIDATE** your child's concern with a statement such as "I bet that worry makes you feel really nervous."

2. **INFORM** your child that the worry is a type of anxiety related to overthinking, too much brain power, or too much of a brain chemical. Phrases like "Your worry is chemical, not factual," or "Smart brains can play tricks on us that make us feel nervous" can be helpful to highlight that worry doesn't mean anything bad will actually happen.

3. **SPEAK CALMLY** and gently. Encourage a few slow, deep breaths: "Let's take some deep breaths to get that brain to relax so the worry can start to fade away."

4. Consider **REFRAMING** your child's worries to highlight a positive value the worry represents: "Being worried about failing your math test is your brain's way of telling you that doing well on the test is important to you."

5. Finally, **REDIRECT** your child's thoughts to either a productive plan to address the worry or a fun, interesting distraction, such as "Let's plan a couple study sessions for that test" or "I need some help planning Grandma's birthday party."

6. Be sure to **AVOID** extensive discussion about the *content* of your child's worry or trying to reason with them about the improbability of the worry. Focusing on the content of the worry will only keep you and your child stuck in an unhelpful (and exhausting) cycle of anxiety and reassurance.

TREATMENT HIGHLIGHTS

- Reassurance does little to reduce worry. Instead, provide age-appropriate psychoeducation about the brain to promote perspective and security.

- Teach relaxation and mindfulness strategies to both kids and parents. Be sure to encourage regularly scheduled "chill time."

- Reframe chronic worry as representing a child's values. Commend children for their conscientiousness.

- Review redirection strategies that can be productive or distracting.

- Consider cognitive-behavioral play therapy for younger worried children.

CHAPTER 12

Caught in the Loop: Interventions for Obsessive-Compulsive Disorder

Parents of anxious kids are often concerned and even distressed about their child's anxiety. However, parents of children struggling with obsessive-compulsive disorder (OCD) may be more than distressed—they may actually be frightened by the hold the disorder has on their child. Indeed, the brains of children with OCD have taken worry to the next level, with obsessive thoughts that can become so intrusive and relentless that the kids become desperate for relief, typically through compulsive behaviors and rituals. Such relief is very temporary and only sustains the cycle of obsessions and compulsions, leaving the kids and their parents feeling helpless.

OCD can take various forms, usually centered around one or more themes, such as preoccupation with order/symmetry, safety, or contamination. One theme that is especially distressing for both kids and parents is the fear of one's own impulses, which causes the kids to be fearful that they will engage in some type of behavior that is harmful to themselves or others. This OCD theme is more common in preteens and adolescents; often, the feared behavior is aggressive or sexual in nature. I once worked with a teen who was consumed by the fear that at some point he would engage in either self-harm or drug use.

Although well-intended, parents' attempts to minimize, reassure, or rationally explain away the obsessive thinking only serve to strengthen it. In fact, some parents—and even therapists—can find themselves becoming a part of the OCD cycle by unintentionally accommodating the OCD rituals. This chapter first focuses on how to provide kids and parents with education about OCD that decreases the fear associated with the disorder. It then offers a variety of child-friendly techniques for empowering children to work their way out of the cycle. The limits of outpatient therapy are also discussed, including when to consider referrals for medication as well as other forms of treatment.

Psychoeducation for Children With OCD and Their Parents

The symptoms of OCD can be especially frightening for kids. The highly persistent nature of OCD convinces children that their mental and behavioral rituals are absolutely essential for preventing catastrophic or horrific events. Translating the scary symptoms of OCD into concrete, nonthreatening language is the first step in effective treatment.

To begin, review the Taking Children on a Journey Through the Brain section in chapter 2 (p. 31). Remind the child, and their parents, that the "protector" part of their brain (i.e., the amygdala) is working much harder than it needs to, which keeps them feeling scared and causes the "manager" part of their brain (the cerebral cortex) to overthink about what they must do to feel safe again. Explain that OCD just means that the child's brain is making it hard to let go of scary or worrisome thoughts and convincing them that they must do certain things to be okay.

For older kids, you can offer a slightly more advanced understanding by defining *obsessions* as thoughts that we cannot seem to get out of our heads and *compulsions* as the things we do to get rid of the thoughts. You can also describe the word *disorder* as "a problem that is very hard or uncomfortable to deal with" and reframe obsessions as representing the child's values (as discussed in chapters 7 and 8). Phrases such as "It's chemical, not factual" or "That's my brain working too hard" can be used to help children create space between their brain and their sense of self. Instruct the parents to use similar phrases to reinforce this process.

Psychoeducation for Preteens/Teens With OCD

Preteens and teens need more in-depth explanations regarding the nature of OCD. Begin by informing them that OCD tends to occur around one or more themes, such as safety, contamination, order/symmetry, or fear of impulses. Next, explain that their particular themes likely represent values that are important to them; for example, a teen with contamination fears likely values being healthy.

If relevant, elaborate on the fear of impulses theme by explaining that some people with OCD obsess about the possibility that they will do something very harmful, usually to themselves or others (e.g., "What if I accidentally kill the dog by dropping a knife in the kitchen?"). Explain that fearing one's own impulses is common among highly conscientious people—in other words, it means they care a lot about others and about doing the right thing ("My fears about the dog show how much I love my pet").

Youths who struggle with OCD may believe that every obsessive occurrence increases the probability of the feared event happening. Such kids essentially believe that their thoughts are nearly equivalent to action—that thinking something is the same as doing it: "I can't stop thinking about throwing up; if I keep thinking about it, it's probably going to happen." This is known as a *probability thought-action fusion* (P-TAF). Informing the client about this phenomenon is essential for countering superstitious thinking and helping combat the often-held belief that something is profoundly wrong with them.

Youths with OCD may also view themselves more negatively from a moral standpoint with every obsessive occurrence, especially impulse-related obsessions: "I must really be a bad person for thinking so much about my dog getting killed." This type of belief is known as a *morality thought-action fusion* (M-TAF). Educating your young clients about the specific ways their OCD presents can help prevent them from internalizing these beliefs (Lewin & Storch, 2017).

Using "Brain Challenges" to Get Kids Out of the Loop

When kids are trapped in an obsessive-compulsive cycle, they often don't recognize what's really going on. I refer to this as an "OCD loop"—an almost continuous cycle that only stops for very short periods of time. Therefore, it's necessary to provide education about OCD *before* attempting direct intervention. You'll know that a child is able to identify their OCD process when they make comments like, "I know it's silly or doesn't make sense, but I just can't help it." Such comments are an opportunity to compliment the child on their awareness: "Excellent job! You're able to identify what's going on with your brain. Now we can work on helping you gradually get out of that OCD loop."

Reducing OCD rituals (let alone eliminating them) is probably one of the most challenging aspects of child anxiety treatment. Various approaches have been developed for this, from cognitive therapies to exposure and response prevention (ERP). However, many children are not yet equipped with adequate metacognition (i.e., thinking about thinking) to practice effective self-talk. In addition, exposure therapy often presents too big a challenge for children with OCD and may prove overwhelming, leaving them feeling more vulnerable. Methods that are not sufficiently tailored to a child's cognitive-developmental level can lead to intense frustration and even panic, which only serves to strengthen their symptoms.

My own frustration with these limitations led me to develop a middle-ground OCD treatment technique that I call "brain challenges." This technique borrows from cognitive-behavioral theory but is less cognitively demanding and does not require the same level of exposure as ERP. The strength of these challenges lies in assisting children with empowering self-talk that challenges their brain to perform their compulsive behavior or ritual in a manner different from their typical procedure. By slightly changing the ritual *every time* they feel compelled to perform it, not only does it become less ritualistic, but the child also experiences incremental empowerment over their impulses. In essence, they are proving to themselves that they can take control of their OCD.

For example, ten-year-old Austin struggles with compulsively arranging items on his bedroom dresser and desk every morning, which results in his being late to school. I asked Austin if he could challenge his brain to place one or two items in a slightly different position or location than he normally would. I encouraged him to use self-talk phrases like "I'm ready to challenge my OCD brain" or "I've got this" while he completed the challenge, and I highlighted his ability to remain in control of his thoughts and actions.

When a ritual involves a certain number of repetitive mental or behavioral actions, encourage the child to choose any alternative number that is less than typical.

After practicing with the child, obtain the child's consent to discuss the brain challenge technique with their parent, and provide the child with the option of having their parent assist them with the challenges at home. Be aware that some children will prefer parental involvement while others will prefer working independently; often this is based on the child's age and disposition.

Creative Corner

An alternative to "fighting" OCD is helping kids develop a playful relationship with the OCD part of their brain. For example, teach lighthearted coping statements like "There goes that OCD brain troll again, telling me what to do. I'm not gonna listen to it—that'll teach it to mess with me!"

When the Therapist Becomes Part of the OCD Ritual

Another challenge in treating childhood OCD is the potential for accommodation—that is, when well-intentioned adults inadvertently enable the avoidance or rituals associated with the condition. While parents are most at risk for accommodation, I learned the hard way that therapists are not immune either.

A fourteen-year-old client of mine, whom I'll call Maria, struggled with a variety of obsessive-compulsive symptoms. She was often consumed by obsessive worry that tended to cycle from theme to theme. Her obsessions ranged from contamination (such as bringing "school germs" into her home) to personal well-being (becoming depressed and suicidal). Maria would bring a handwritten list of multiple obsessions to every session and ask me if any of them were actually valid or representative of OCD. Initially, this seemed like a helpful exercise to distinguish legitimate worries from irrational obsessions. However, her list only grew over time, and she became increasingly dependent on me for clarification and reassurance that all of her concerns were related to OCD. Eventually, I realized that I had become part of her ritual.

After an open discussion about this situation, I used the brain challenge technique to help Maria present fewer concerns and in different formats (going from handwritten to digital, and eventually from memory). I then gave her options for how I could respond in more subtle ways to her concerns—we started with verbal statements, later moved to gestures, and finally silence with redirection to another topic. By working together to change up her ritual, we were gradually able to defuse its power and spend our session on more productive conversation.

Preventing Parental Pitfalls With Your Child's OCD

When your child is struggling with the intense fears and behavioral or mental compulsions that are a part of OCD, your first impulse may be to reassure your child, whether by minimizing or rationally explaining away their obsessive thinking (e.g., "You don't need to worry about tornadoes—we haven't had a bad tornado in this area for decades!") or by overly accommodating their rituals ("Sure, I'll go around with you and we'll make sure all the doors are locked"). This is a common (and understandable) response for parents. However, with OCD, such reassurance is not only ineffective but counterproductive—it actually *strengthens* your child's obsessive thinking and compulsions.

The following are some more effective approaches to helping your child manage their OCD symptoms:

- Remind your child of the science behind OCD to help them create space between their brain and their sense of self. Model and prompt your child to use phrases like "It's chemical, not factual" or "That's just my brain working too hard."

- Reframe your child's worries in terms of their values. For example: "Your fear that you might hurt the dog shows how much you love her and want to take the very best care of her."

- If your child is able to recognize when they're stuck in an OCD loop, compliment them on their awareness: "Excellent job! You're getting better at figuring out what's going on with your brain. Now we can work on helping you get out of that OCD loop." Support them in practicing their "brain challenges" or other skills recommended by their mental health provider.

- Encourage your child to use positive self-talk to increase their confidence. This can include phrases like "I'm ready to challenge my OCD brain" or "I've got this!"

- Help your child develop a playful relationship with the "OCD part" of their brain. This might include lighthearted coping statements like "There goes that OCD brain troll again, telling me what to do. I'm not gonna listen to it—that'll teach it to mess with me!"

Using these ideas and the guidance of your child's mental health provider, complete the following sentence prompts to better identify how you may inadvertently be strengthening your child's OCD symptoms, as well as how you can better assist your child in the future.

1. When my child talks about obsessive thoughts, I tend to _____

_____.

    Instead, I will attempt to _____

_____.

2. When I see my child engaging in compulsive or ritualistic behavior, I will _____

_____

    rather than _____

_____.

3. My concern and distress about my child can cause me to say or do _____

_____.

    However, I will work on saying or doing _____

_____ instead.

4. When I become frustrated or irritated with my child's OCD symptoms, I will try to remember

_____

_____

    in order to prevent _____

_____.

Talking Back to My OCD Brain

OCD brains think way too much about the same things over and over. When this happens, you might feel like your brain is forcing you to do a certain thing in order to stop something really bad from happening. Once you've done what your brain told you to do, the thoughts might go away—but the really tricky thing is, those thoughts always come back, whether it's right away or later on.

Next time, instead of doing what your OCD brain says, talk back to it. Fill in the following sentences to challenge your OCD brain. By doing something different from what your OCD brain tells you to do, you'll start feeling more confident because now *you're* the one in charge!

"You need to _____ _____ or else _____ _____ will happen!"

"NO! I'm going to _____ _____ instead, and I know it's going to be just fine."

Breaking Free of Compulsive Device Usage

Self-control with digital devices is a challenge for many adults, let alone children, whose self-control is still in development. For some children, especially those prone to OCD, device usage can become all-encompassing. What follows is a step-by-step method for helping children and parents work together to begin breaking free of compulsive device usage. First, before an actual device usage schedule can be developed, explore the specific nature of the child's usage. (See the guidance on effective device management, p. 57.)

Different activities and platforms meet varying needs—for example, social media posting is associated with a strong need for social recognition, while gaming may reflect a need for mastery and control. Several therapeutic conversations may be necessary to determine the specific needs being met by the child's preferred technological activities. Knowing these needs is vital because they have implications for the types of "real-world" activities that can serve as meaningful substitutes for the child's virtual activities.

Next, assess the emotional and cognitive states that trigger the child's device usage. For example, do they turn to their phone out of boredom, sadness, or loneliness? Perhaps endless scrolling on TikTok signifies the youth's need for some fun with their friends. Also identify the dominant thoughts and feelings while the youth is technologically engaged. Do they display excitement, joy, or rage while using the device? Are they zoned out?

Be sure to consider the role of escapism, as many kids may use devices as a way to escape the demands and stressors of their daily lives. These kids may benefit from supportive adults who can empathize with their stressed-out state and work with them to reduce stressors and bolster effective coping skills. Research is growing on the effects of prolonged device usage, especially in virtual reality formats. The term *digital dissociation* is being used to describe experiences including depersonalization or derealization during which individuals "zone out" and may experience a blurred distinction between their online and offline lives (Peckmann et al., 2022).

Further complicating the problem of excessive device usage is the lack of restraint that can occur when people communicate online rather than in person. This phenomenon, referred to as "the online disinhibition effect," can lead to both youths and adults engaging in negative online behaviors such as trolling and cyberbullying. Today's parents must not only be keenly aware of their children's device usage but also recognize that kids are participating in various virtual communities and interacting in ways that may depart significantly from their offline relationships (Suler, 2006). Sadly, my clinical work has included cases in which cyberbullying has led to real-life violence in schools and psychological scarring that ultimately ended in a teen's death by suicide.

Once you have a solid understanding of the psychological factors at play, you can begin helping the child develop a schedule for using their device. First, assess the typical daily and weekly amount of device usage by speaking separately with the parents and child. Next, assist the parents in creating an initial, tentative schedule for their child's device usage (as described in chapter 5). A good place to start is by identifying acceptable time slots during the week for the child to use devices. The amount of time for each "usage episode" should be slightly less than the current average; for example, if a child is typically using devices for three consecutive hours, then suggest two and a half hours.

Encourage the parents to start by presenting their child with options that are likely to be acceptable to them. For instance, continuing the previous scenario, the parents can ask their child whether they would prefer to reduce their usage episode by half an hour or by one hour. Their answer will be obvious, but the perception of control is critical. For kids who are older and more savvy, encourage the parents to offer a genuine choice if possible. For example, they might maintain that their child is limited to 17.5 hours of (nonacademic) device time per week, but allow the child to choose whether they would like 2.5 hours every day of the week or 1.5 hours on weekdays and 5 hours on Saturday and Sunday.

Brainstorm with both the parents and child about potential substitute activities to replace time previously spent on devices. The substitute activities must be enjoyable to the child—homework and chores are not options. Help both parties come up with experiences that meet the previously determined needs and promote a positive emotional state.

To prevent kids from seeing their parents as hypocritical, encourage the parents to model self-control with their own devices. It's also beneficial to establish "no-tech" times for the entire family to participate in group interaction or activities.

Over time, as real life rather than virtual life becomes more engaging, assist parents and kids in continuing to reduce, streamline, and add additional structure to their device usage. Remember that the ultimate goal is to help the child meet the needs that are being met online via real-world alternatives. Also be alert to any signs of regression; these may signal a change in the child's psychological state, which can then be addressed therapeutically.

TIPS WITH TEENS

- Not all device usage is the same, especially with teens. Devices serve numerous functions in a teen's life, from education and research to self-expression and socializing.

- Explore with teens what types of device usage they find most challenging to regulate, and which ones seem to have positive and negative effects on their anxiety or mood. Then empower them to make healthy adjustments.

- Encourage parents to avoid lecturing or complaining to teens about their device usage. Instead, assist them in developing strategies for engaging their child in exploratory discussions that can give the parents a better understanding of their teen's virtual life.

Limitations of Outpatient Treatment for OCD

Recognizing our limits as therapists isn't always easy, but it is indeed necessary. Despite our carefully thought-out and well-executed interventions, sometimes our efforts cannot adequately compete with every child's brain chemistry. Acknowledging the limits of weekly outpatient therapy is critical so that alternative treatments can be explored.

Keep in mind that brains have very strong practice effects, so the same neural pathways tend to be activated again and again. For kids with OCD, this means that untreated symptoms become more ingrained with every passing month, causing increasing distress and impairment over time.

While there is no definitive guideline, I become concerned when two to three months of consistent therapy produces very few gains. Consistently inadequate progress signals the likely need for a medication consultation.

When interfacing with concerned parents and perpetually distressed kids, consider starting with a gentle discussion about the risks of *not* considering medication. If you feel qualified to engage in this type of discussion, explore the parents' beliefs, attitudes, and previous experiences regarding the use of psychiatric medication. If you do not feel qualified, refer parents to *credible* sources on this topic (as medication myths run rampant) and refer them for psychiatric evaluation and consultation as needed.

Other treatment options for more severe levels of OCD include intensive outpatient programs, which meet daily for several hours with a team approach, and residential or inpatient treatment programs. While some clients will need a different type of treatment than what you are able to offer alone, initiating compassionate conversations with these kids and their families can pave the way for their eventual relief from OCD.

TREATMENT HIGHLIGHTS

- Provide thorough, age-appropriate psychoeducation on OCD to kids and parents. Be sure to include relevant themes and thought-action fusion.

- Use reframing to highlight a child's values and conscientiousness.

- Employ challenge ladders to assist with exposure and desensitization. Use brain challenges (continuous response modification) to combat rigid ritualism.

- Be mindful of the pitfalls of both parent and therapist accommodation.

- Equip kids with empowering self-talk.

- Explore the psychological needs and emotional or cognitive factors of a child's compulsive device usage before developing a usage schedule.

- Consider medication referrals and other alternatives to outpatient therapy for treatment-resistant OCD.

CHAPTER 13

"I'm So Awkward": Overcoming Social Anxiety Disorder

Every generation has its psychological strengths and challenges, which are shaped by the unique events and circumstances of their early lives. For Generation Z and, more recently, Generation Alpha, social anxiety has become a prominent issue. Members of Gen Z, or "Zoomers," were born between 1997 and 2012. One of the largest and most diverse generations so far in the United States, they essentially grew up with smartphones; as a result, they spend more time online than previous generations and are often referred to as "digital natives" (Nagy, 2017).

In her book *iGen*, psychologist Jean Twenge highlights how Gen Z is poorly prepared for adulthood (Twenge, 2017). Factors such as excessive screen time, sleep deprivation, and a pervasive societal focus on safety have promoted a generation of risk-averse youth hindered by anxiety and depression. Such emotional challenges have contributed to a delayed adulthood for many in Gen Z. Interestingly, adolescence lasts three times longer than it used to, according to psychologist Laurence Steinberg (2015).

Generation Alpha, born from 2010 to the present, is more technology-immersed than any generation before, and is thus sometimes referred to as the "Glass Generation." Raised by Millennials, Gen Alpha kids are very likely to have an online presence from birth. Such early digital documentation of their lives may foster a very strong need for recognition coupled with intense self-consciousness. With the social media world (both locally and globally) at their fingertips, Gen Alphas are the most socially connected—but also the most socially anxious—generation (McCrindle & Fell, 2021).

Perhaps it's no wonder that I hear phrases like "I'm so awkward" and "That's so cringe-worthy" from many of my young clients now. These statements may reflect a heightened sense of self-consciousness, even paranoia at times, that seems to go beyond the previous developmental norms of youth. In fact, social anxiety disorder is on the rise and has only been fueled by the COVID-19 pandemic. About 10 percent of young adults and teens in the US have social anxiety, and the problem is also growing among younger children (Hofmann & DiBartolo, 2014). Psychologists across the country expect the disorder to become even more prevalent and lead to more instances of depression.

We all know the vital role socialization plays in contributing to a child's psychological well-being. Perhaps more than ever, we need our children to form healthy in-person connections with both peers and adults. With that goal in mind, this chapter aims to equip socially anxious children with a renewed sense of confidence in their ability to communicate face-to-face and to feel good about their relationships.

Preparing Socially Anxious Children for Treatment

Kids and teens with social anxiety vary widely in their readiness for therapy. As clinicians, we should recognize that simply talking to a mental health provider is a huge step for them. I have found the following step-by-step approach helpful for easing into the process of social anxiety treatment.

First, commend your young client for addressing their social anxiety. Point out how simply talking to you about their issue is a courageous and important first step. Also inform them that their generation tends to struggle more with social anxiety, so they are certainly not alone. In fact, they likely have friends and peers with the same challenges, whether they know it or not.

Next, promote conversation about low-demand topics such as preferred activities and interests. Be sure to encourage discussion about their virtual world, including their favorite YouTubers, video games, and social platforms. Remember, the initial goal is to provide them with a type of corrective experience, meaning a comfortable face-to-face interchange that they were likely worried about.

You will likely hear the word "awkward" in reference to how they perceive their in-person social experiences. Explain that *feeling* awkward is not the same as *being* awkward. I like giving obvious, humorous examples of true social awkwardness, such as asking someone they just met about their favorite cheese, farm animal, or planet!

Look for opportunities to provide relevant psychoeducation. For example, I tend to discuss how social anxiety can take one or more forms. Self-conscious thoughts like *They're going to think I'm weird*, avoidant behavior like looking at the ground, and physiological signs such as feeling flushed, sweaty, or nauseous are all common expressions of social anxiety. In addition, highlight how these symptoms are actually due to their brain's amygdala or "protector," which increases chemicals/hormones such as adrenaline and cortisol that can make their mind and body feel really uncomfortable.

As you explore your client's social anxiety symptoms, eventually inquire as to which ones are most upsetting. For example, I find some kids become intensely self-conscious when they become flushed or sweaty, while others experience racing self-critical thoughts or suddenly feel nauseous and perhaps even fear vomiting or other intense panic reactions. Your treatment can be guided by which symptom type they wish to address first. Keep in mind that kids with a long-term history of intense physiological symptoms are most likely to benefit from a medication evaluation.

Understanding and Empowering Your Socially Anxious Child

As the parent of a socially anxious child, you have likely tried reasoning with them about how they are overthinking social situations, telling them they are not truly "awkward" and highlighting that they'd feel much better if they would just get to know more people. Nevertheless, their social anxiety remains intact. Below are some points to consider in order to help your socially anxious child feel understood, as well as some suggestions for starting conversations that might help them gradually become less avoidant and more proactive.

- Talk to your child about what kinds of negative outcomes they think could occur in a social situation. Then ask them to reflect on the number of times such events have actually occurred.

- Ask them whether they frequently judge others negatively in social situations. If so, how long do they continue to think this way? The goal is to illustrate that most people are not holding on to negative perceptions of others for any significant length of time.

- Remind them that as humans, we tend to mainly think about ourselves rather than fixating on others. Our thoughts about other people in social situations are usually fleeting; our brains always revert back to our own thoughts and feelings.

- Ask them to reflect on their social media usage. What kinds of messages are they receiving? What are their observations about people's online communication?

- Explain that social media tends to bring out extreme, exaggerated, or distorted views rather than reflecting more moderate and likely more realistic perceptions of others. Have them reflect on the differences in their online versus in-person social communication.

- Encourage your child to work with their mental health provider to develop a plan for gradually managing and decreasing social anxiety. Offer to participate in this work to the degree your child prefers.

Quick Commenting: Getting Out of Your Head and Into the World

Social anxiety keeps us trapped in our heads, often thinking one negative thought after another about ourselves in comparison to others: *I'm so weird and awkward. I don't know what to say, so I won't say anything. I'd probably just say something stupid anyway.*

We sometimes think that people without social anxiety always know exactly what to say, how to say it, and when to say it. But in fact, such people simply think *less* about what's in their head before they say it. Most of the time, what they say turns out just fine. However, those with social anxiety overthink before they speak, leading them to often say nothing or perhaps mumble a few words. This leaves them feeling awkward and isolated.

The goal for young people with social anxiety is to get their thoughts out of their head and into the world more quickly. It may seem a bit scary at first; trusting yourself is key. Know that your brain isn't likely to allow you to say something that's *really* odd. People with that tendency are verbally impulsive, something that is not associated with social anxiety.

Now is the time to practice speaking quickly. Here are some tips to help you practice:

- Spend some time with someone you trust and notice how you tend to just say whatever comes to your mind. Notice that what comes out of your mouth is totally appropriate.

- Next, speak with your therapist and ask to practice this type of "quick commenting" during your next session.

- Finally, look for opportunities to say what's in your head to others with whom you are usually quiet. The more you do, the more confident you'll become!

"Association-to-Dialogue" Technique for Social Anxiety

Earlier, I mentioned that social anxiety treatment essentially provides a corrective experience for intensely self-conscious kids who may seldom experience comfortable in-person communication about themselves. With that in mind, here is a step-by-step method I find both fun and useful for getting clients more comfortable with verbal spontaneity. Use this in conjunction with the Quick Commenting handout (p. 138).

- **Simple word association:** Inform your client that being more verbally spontaneous can eventually help decrease social anxiety. Ask them to quickly say the first thing that comes to mind after you say a word. If they hesitate, playfully tell them they are thinking too hard and move on to another word. Keep the pace quick and the tone light, like a game.

- **Observation association:** Once your client has mastered word association, ask them to look around your room or office. Tell them that you will eventually say "Now," which will be their signal to quickly make a comment about anything in the room. Once they do so, respond conversationally. For example, your client says, "That orange lamp is interesting." You respond, "Yes, the lampshade is made of a mineral called mica. I really like the orange glow it gives off."

- **Observation association with a question:** Repeat the previous step, but this time, inform your client to ask a question rather than make a comment about something in the room. Then answer their question in a manner that promotes conversation. If they say or ask anything else, continue the conversation for a bit.

- **Comment/question about the therapist:** This is usually the most challenging part for clients, so proceed after you notice they have become relatively comfortable and more verbally spontaneous. Inform your client that you would like them to either make a comment or ask a question that relates to you. Wait a few seconds, then say "Now." If they hesitate, explore the obstacle and repeat earlier steps. Once spontaneity resumes, try again. Respond naturally, asking them questions or making comments in response. Eventually, conversation will be flowing with more ease. Empower them by highlighting their emerging competence!

Combating Outcome Certainty

Many socially anxious children are very risk-averse, which can deprive them of positive experiences and delay their emergence into adulthood. Over the past few years, I have noticed a strong avoidance in teens facing upcoming transitions or milestones, such as obtaining a driver's license or applying for their first job: "What if I fail my road test?" "What if my manager is really rude?"

I use the term *outcome certainty* to describe a client's preoccupation with a guaranteed positive outcome as a requirement for initiative or action. For example, a teen who wants a job but avoids looking for a job may worry that she will end up disliking something about the job, or that something about the job will go poorly.

Once I recognized and named this phenomenon, I realized that labeling wasn't enough; I needed to do something about it! Borrowing from various cognitive therapies, I developed the following process for helping anxious clients combat outcome certainty so that they can begin approaching rather than avoiding healthy risks.

First, I explore the meaning of the client's perceived potentially negative outcomes. For example, if they got a job and made a mistake, what would that mean? Often, these clients make negative personal attributions such as "It would mean that I'm just an idiot." While it's tempting to respond with "No, you're actually very smart," this would likely prove ineffective. Instead, I'll take their statement and apply it universally: "If you're an idiot, are all people who make mistakes while learning a new job idiots? If so, then I guess I'm an idiot as well." Of course, a little humor and a light touch go a long way.

Next, I normalize the outcome and separate it from the client's identity and self-worth. I also speak a step removed, referring to people in general rather than the client: "Making mistakes is necessary for everyone in a new job in order to learn. Plus, good managers expect mistakes, especially early in the job. Those mistakes come with learning and have nothing to do with us as people. It's a task, not a reflection of intelligence." This is essentially a form of cognitive restructuring. However, recognize that your client may need more validation and anxiety-management skill-building if they appear resistant.

Once my client is receptive to new thought patterns, I reframe any possible negative outcome as both positive and useful: "If you make mistakes, it shows that you are serious about learning the job and doing it well. Plus, you learned valuable information that can help you going forward."

Finally, we collaboratively set a time frame for a commitment to a small first step. For example, "Let's talk about a simple first step, such as doing some research on what jobs are available in your community. What day and time could you commit to doing some research on that?" Assess and commend any level of progress and identify any obstacles. Then repeat the previous steps and set another small goal. Consider a less demanding goal if resistance or avoidance continues.

Treating Social Media Distress via Functional Mood Analysis

Social media is often a significant catalyst and reinforcer of social anxiety. Heavy social media usage has also been shown to correlate with depression, especially in youths (Twenge, 2020). However, advocating for parents to simply restrict teens from social media use prevents an exploration of the factors contributing to emotional distress.

Instead, empower teens to do their own assessment of how their social media usage affects them emotionally. I use the term *functional mood analysis* (FMA) to describe the process of evaluating how social media and emotional states are related to and affect each other. Once a teen understands this relationship through their own analysis, they are more likely to begin self-regulating their social media usage. Teach your young clients FMA using the following steps:

- First, encourage the client to track their anxiety, mood, or other emotional state over the course of each day for one week. Ask them to note any social media usage before, during, and after these mood states.

- Ask about the nature of their usage: Are they posting videos, checking for likes/views, chatting with friends, social gaming, or something else?

- Next, encourage them to reflect on their motivation each time they use social media. Do they have certain expectations? Are these expectations being met? After a week, ask them to review their notes and look for any patterns they notice regarding their emotions and their usage. Encourage them to bring their observations to session in written or digital format.

- Finally, promote discussion about any noteworthy patterns they discover. Assist them by speculating about the implications of these patterns, and ask whether they would like to make a change of some kind. For example: "So, you found out that each night you look for positive comments on your Instagram posts, and how well you sleep depends on whether you received enough. That's a great insight. What do you think about it? Do you think any change in your social media routine could help you sleep better?"

Ultimately, the goal is for teens to understand the connection between their social media usage and mood states, and to consider the kinds of changes that could improve their emotional and physical well-being.

TIPS WITH TEENS

- Assist teens in discovering the kinds of needs they are trying to meet with their social media usage. Can any of these needs be met in other ways?

- Explore any conclusions they have come to about how social media affects themselves and their peers emotionally. Do they have any ideas for how to address negative emotional outcomes for themselves and their friends?

- Gently encourage teens to reflect on their social media self-control. Are they feeling more or less in control over time?

TREATMENT HIGHLIGHTS

- Ease kids and teens into social anxiety treatment via low-demand conversation.

- Provide psychoeducation about social anxiety, including how it is more common in their generation.

- Assess the most distressing social anxiety symptoms to determine whether to initially focus on cognitive, behavioral, or physiological interventions.

- Use the "association-to-dialogue" and "quick commenting" techniques to promote verbal spontaneity and social confidence.

- Consider the influence of outcome certainty and use cognitive restructuring as needed.

- Employ a functional mood analysis (FMA) to promote changes for improved emotional functioning.

CHAPTER 14

When Anxiety Acts Out: Managing Anxiety-Fueled Misbehavior

Our society tends to hyperfocus on children's behavior, which is useful to a degree. (Misbehavior is, quite frankly, annoying, often leading to an impatient search for a quick fix.) But often, such hyperfocus leads the adults in children's lives to overlook the environmental, neurological, developmental, social, and emotional factors that fuel what we label "misbehavior." As a result, we can become consumed with behavior modification without adequate attention to other aspects of the child.

While most adults have a good amount of empathy for anxious kids who present as worried, fearful, or panic-stricken, the same cannot be said for kids whose anxiety manifests less as distress and more as disruption. Maintaining empathy for kids who display disruptive behavior is indeed a challenge, but it is vital to address the underlying contributors that result in this behavior.

As clinicians, we often hear parents and teachers use the term *oppositional defiant* to describe difficult, noncompliant kids. It's important to bear in mind that any of the anxiety disorders previously discussed may ultimately be responsible for a child's oppositional defiance.

This chapter will challenge you to discover the possible underlying types of anxiety contributing to behaviors that are extremely challenging (and downright unpleasant) for the adults in these children's lives. The worksheets and handouts are designed to help anxious, disruptive children feel better understood and to equip their parents to effectively manage disruptive behavior.

Going Beyond Oppositional Defiant Disorder

Certain diagnoses garner a lot of attention; oppositional defiant disorder (ODD) is definitely one of them. We still live in a society that strongly values obedience in children (e.g., "Listen and do as you are told"). While some kids are oppositional by nature, others are oppositional due to distress. As clinicians, we must safeguard against fully buying into an ODD diagnosis until a thorough assessment is completed. Research shows that kids with true ODD tend to enjoy provoking anger in others. These kids are not simply uncooperative, but rather plan and implement clever tactics designed to irritate or anger others so they can get what they want. Genuine ODD is often a precursor to conduct disorder in adolescents.

Many children diagnosed with ODD do not actually meet such criteria. Instead, we find that these noncompliant kids are actually worried, fearful, obsessive, avoidant, and therefore desperately preoccupied with maintaining control. The key to reducing their oppositional and defiant behavior lies in alleviating the accompanying anxiety so that relinquishing control becomes possible for the child.

With this type of client, begin by building rapport as you would with any child. However, rapport-building is admittedly more challenging with disruptive children. Discovering the child's agenda is often a necessary first step: What is this kid trying to accomplish or avoid? Simple questions such as "What do you want to see happen?" can yield information about the child's actual intentions. Similarly, questions such as "What do you want to make sure doesn't happen?" can reveal what situations or occurrences the child wishes to avoid.

Once you have an understanding of the child's agenda, validate their need to control in an empathetic manner: "So you want to make sure that you get a turn to be the leader."

Eventually, go further when you recognize how anxiety plays a role: "Maybe you're concerned that if you don't say anything, you will never get a chance to be the leader."

Now it's time to obtain consent from the child so that you can inform their parents about the true nature of the disruptive behavior at hand. The goal is to instill both awareness and empathy in the parents so that effective response strategies can be implemented. Such strategies must include validation, limits, and appropriate options or alternatives for the child. Essentially, "disruptively distressed" kids need to feel understood, need limits, and need acceptable options for expressing themselves. Think of this as a form of empathetic limit-setting that includes other options to help the child get their needs met to some degree. I call this the *Go With the VLO* method, where VLO stands for *validate*, *limit*, and *option*. Using this approach, a parent could speak to an acting-out child by saying something like: "I understand you want to be the leader, but today is Maya's turn. However, I will give you a chance to be a helper after lunch, and to be a leader later this week."

Creative Corner

Anxious, disruptive kids need healthy outlets to channel their inner restlessness, but too often the adults in their lives simply try to squelch their misbehavior. Consider brainstorming with the child's parents and teachers to find prosocial or productive tasks at home or school that could help the child defuse their inner tension and strengthen their sense of worth.

When Anxiety Gets Me in Trouble

Anxiety can make us think and feel many different things. Strong feelings like anger, fear, and embarrassment can make us have very negative thoughts and lead us into trouble. Learning about which feelings cause which thoughts, and which thoughts cause which behaviors, can help us get in trouble a lot less.

Use this exercise to figure out what feelings and thoughts get you in trouble, and what you can do differently. For ideas of what you could do, see the Coping Activity Ideas handout (p. 146) or ask your therapist to help you brainstorm.

When I'm **angry,**	I think:	and then I	☐ Hit or kick ☐ Throw ☐ Yell ☐ Run ☐
But instead, when I'm angry I could:			
When I'm **scared,**	I think:	and then I	☐ Hit or kick ☐ Hide ☐ Scream ☐ Run ☐
But instead, when I'm scared I could:			
When I'm **embarrassed,**	I think:	and then I	☐ Hit or kick ☐ Cry ☐ Yell ☐ Run ☐
But instead, when I'm embarrassed I could:			

Coping Activity Ideas*

Sometimes it can be hard to think of what might help you feel better when you're feeling scared, embarrassed, angry, or other overwhelming emotions. Listed below are some activities that kids often find helpful (and even fun!). You can also add your own ideas to the list or ask your therapist for help brainstorming.

- Punch a pillow
- Take slow, deep breaths
- Do jumping jacks
- Use a fidget toy or worry stone
- Listen to music
- Dance
- Write about your feelings
- Draw or color
- Watch a funny video
- Squeeze a stress ball
- Read a book
- Play with a pet
- Ask a loved one for a hug

- Stretch or do yoga
- Notice what you see, hear, feel, smell, and taste
- Make a cozy spot to relax
- Drink cold water or hot cocoa
- Play a game
- Spend time outside
- Write a story, poem, or song
- Talk to someone you trust
- Write down what's bothering you, then rip it up
- Write or say aloud some positive things about yourself
- Ask someone you trust for help

---

* Many of these suggestions are based on Janine Halloran's *Coping Skills for Kids Workbook* (2018).

Discovering the Feelings That Fuel My Child's Misbehavior

When your child misbehaves, it may seem reasonable to reprimand, punish, or lecture them. However, doing so is often ineffective, and it overlooks the possible causes of the behavior. Sometimes kids act out not because they want to hurt or inconvenience others, but simply because they're feeling scared, embarrassed, or angry and don't know how to cope with these anxiety-related feelings.

Complete the sentences below to reflect on possible anxieties that could be leading your child to behave inappropriately. Then, try the **VLO method**—that is: **v**alidate your child's feelings, set a **l**imit, and provide another **o**ption. Consistently "going with the VLO" can significantly reduce your child's disruptive behavior over time and improve your relationship with them.

If you need help brainstorming healthy coping options to offer your child, see the Coping Activity Ideas handout (p. 146) or ask your child's mental health provider for guidance.

1. When my child acts aggressively (e.g., hits or throws something), it might mean they feel _____

   _____.

   I can say, "I understand you're feeling _____, but it's not okay to

   _____. Instead, you can

   _____ or _____."

2. When my child yells or screams, it might mean they feel _____.

   I can say, "I understand you're feeling _____, but it's not okay to

   _____. Instead, you can

   _____ or _____."

3. When my child runs off or hides, it might mean they feel _____.

   I can say, "I understand you're feeling _____, but it's not okay to

   _____. Instead, you can

   _____ or _____."

Reframing How Parents Think About Misbehavior and Adolescent "Disrespect"

Misbehavior is not only a typical concern for parents but also a trigger for feeling disrespected and manipulated. Parents tend to personalize their children's misbehavior rather than see it as a reflection of anxiety or distress. When they do so, they become increasingly angered with the child, which prevents a more accurate understanding of the child's emotional state. In her book *Beyond Behaviors*, psychologist Mona Delahooke writes, "When we see a behavior that is problematic or confusing, the first question we should ask isn't 'How do we get rid of it?' but rather 'What is this telling us about the child?'" (Delahooke, 2019, p. 11). Shifting the parent's focus from the behavior to the feeling can reduce their anger and promote both empathy and a more effective response.

Before reframing highly challenging behavior, be sure to validate the parent's anger, frustration, fatigue, and helplessness. Also be aware that parents of highly disruptive children often feel considerable guilt and inadequacy, especially those who have received criticism and judgment from others, sometimes even from close friends and family. I tend to discourage parents from evaluating their parental skills or worth based on their anxious child's challenging behavior. I can still hear my internship supervisor's words: "Many parents enter your office with a million failures, so be gentle and confront them with care."

Here are some phrases I find useful for helping parents adopt a more accurate and balanced view of their child, especially when they are feeling highly frustrated or fragile and largely to blame:

- "Your child's just wired that way."

  This comment highlights the child's natural predisposition so the parents can be reminded that genetics plays a big role. In other words, parents aren't to blame.

- "It's about them, not about you."

  Reduce parents' tendency to personalize their child's behavior and instead view it simply as the child's own agenda. This decreases parents' feelings of anger and disrespect.

- "Sure, your child is manipulative, just like the rest of us. We all tend to try to get what we want."

  Assist parents in viewing manipulation as more normal and less negative. You can also highlight that such children are particularly intelligent.

- "The intensity of this behavior reflects the intensity of their anxiety."

  This type of statement shifts parents' focus from the problematic behavior to understanding the emotional state of their child. This helps promote empathy and facilitates communication skill-building and behavior management.

Parents of teens are usually especially sensitive to feeling disrespected by them. It's understandable, given how verbally volatile some teens can be when they are highly distressed. Remind parents that teens' brains are still developing, particularly in the regions that have to do with emotional self-control. Anxious teens who tend to be verbally impulsive are more likely to express their anxiety as agitation, anger, and irritability without regard for how the other person is receiving them.

Using the Rewind Method With "Disrespectful" Kids

As a parent, do you ever wish you had a remote control for your child's less than pleasant comments? Until that tool is invented, here's a step-by-step approach for responding to and managing unwelcome "disrespectful" statements from your kid.

- Express your feelings, not judgment. For example, rather than stating "You're being disrespectful—you *cannot* speak to me like that!" say:

    "What you've just said doesn't feel good to me."

- Identify your child's emotional state (e.g., frustration, anger, disappointment, or desperation), then label this emotion for them:

    "It seems like you're really frustrated right now and unhappy with my decision."

- Wait to hear their response to see if they confirm or clarify their feelings. Restate how they are feeling if necessary, then provide validation:

    "I understand how frustrated you are by my decision."

- Ask them to "rewind" and restate their initial remark, this time with reference to how they are truly feeling and using a tactful and respectful tone. For example:

    "I'm really frustrated that you won't let me hang out with my friends tonight."

    Be sure to model the emotional tone that fits the feeling but also conveys a sense of respect.

- Once your kid has appropriately expressed their feelings, show appreciation for their doing so:

    "Thank you for cooperating and speaking more accurately and respectfully."

- If your child refuses to restate, calmly ask them again to do so, but disengage if they continue to refuse:

    "When you're ready to speak differently to me, let me know."

    Your kid will likely want to have the last word, and while it's tempting to come back at them, remember that your "last word" is walking away.

- Once your kid cooperates, you may be able to have a conversation that ultimately leads to increased mutual understanding and possibly some type of contingency agreement, problem-solving, or compromise.

TREATMENT HIGHLIGHTS

- Identify potential anxiety contributors fueling oppositional and defiant child behaviors.

- Kids with generalized anxiety disorder (GAD) or obsessive-compulsive disorder (OCD) often exhibit manipulative behavior to avoid feeling anxious and to maintain control.

- Challenging children need just as much validation and understanding of their thoughts and feelings as do those who are distressed but much less disruptive.

- Use empathetic limit-setting such as the "Go With the VLO" method.

- Help children develop awareness of how some of their anxious thoughts and feelings can get them in trouble, then promote healthy alternatives.

- After validating parental anger or feelings of inadequacy, reframe the child's misbehavior in terms of the child's feelings to promote greater empathy and understanding, which can lead to more effective outcomes.

CHAPTER 15

Stressed Out at School: Managing Anxiety in the Classroom

Children are facing increased academic demands at earlier ages, and both kids and parents are feeling the pressure. Teachers are also stressed, as they are often expected to produce high-scoring students without adequate resources or support.

Kids and families are paying a price for this early emphasis on academic achievement. Research suggests that young children are at increased risk for anxiety over time when academic achievement takes precedence over other developmental needs, such as socialization and self-regulation (Sparks, 2007). Moreover, while an early focus on academic achievement may have some benefit, a persistent expectation of high achievement can ultimately lead to perfectionism, burnout, anxiety, and depression.

This chapter focuses on assisting students who are struggling with school-related anxiety. Several teacher tips are included to address common areas of concern, such as test anxiety and homework avoidance. These handouts can be shared with educators, parents, school counselors, and other staff for assisting children in the school setting. Keep in mind that students may be dealing with one or more of the anxiety disorders that have been addressed in this book. When this is the case, collaboration between mental health providers and educators is even more critical to promote the child's psychological and academic functioning.

Relationship-Building With Anxious Students

One of a teacher's most effective tools for assisting anxious students is connection, which occurs largely through effective communication. Here are some tips for building a calmer connection with distressed students:

- Be mindful of your voice volume, as sensitive students may misinterpret you.

- Use a reassuring but confident tone of voice.

- Compliment and correct without an audience.

- When providing corrective feedback, validate before instructing.

- Avoid cheerleading; for example, say "Do what you can" versus "Do your best."

Reframing the Three D's: Defiance, Disrespect, and Disruption

Some anxious children are easy to identify: They are the ones who express worry and fear or are tearful or avoidant. However, other kids express anxiety through irritability, agitation, and misbehavior. Such children are often referred to as defiant, disrespectful, and disruptive. These labels can foster a self-fulfilling prophecy—as adults continue to view a child through this lens, not only does the child's anxiety grow, but misbehavior often escalates as well. Thus, it's essential to recognize the emotional factors fueling children's behavior. Consider the following:

- **Defiance** may reflect frustration and irritability associated with a need for control. *Try providing the child with choices whenever possible.* For example, allowing children to decide whether to complete odd or even numbered items on a worksheet, or offering flexible seating options, can promote some sense of control and may foster more cooperation.

- **Disrespect** is often fueled by distress associated with feeling disregarded and misunderstood. *It's important to listen carefully, validate the child's concerns, and provide them with a socially appropriate alternative for expressing themselves:*

  "I understand that you're angry and disappointed that you can't be the line leader today, but instead of yelling, take a deep breath and use a calm voice to say, 'I'm mad about not being the line leader.'"

- **Disruption** may represent feeling restless, bored, or overwhelmed. *Consider providing children exhibiting such behavior with prosocial tasks, additional schoolwork, or responsibilities but in a nonpunitive way:*

  "It looks like you might need something else to do; would you like some more math problems or do you want to help me put these books back on the shelf?"

Creating a Calm and Responsive Classroom

Just as a child's home environment plays a major role in either contributing to or reducing anxiety, so does the classroom. Below are tips for creating and maintaining a calm and responsive learning environment.

- Consider beginning each day with a routine that both engages and prepares students for learning.

- Whenever possible, incorporate peaceful music and soft lighting.

- Provide an area for self-regulation, such as a "calm corner" with materials that promote self-soothing.

- To avoid abrupt transitions, use rituals to ease children from one activity to another.

- For transitions with multiple steps, use numbers or colors to represent the onset of a new behavior. For example, "When I say 1, everyone stand up" and "When I say 2, come to the gathering area and sit down."

- Rather than "calling out" distracted students, establish nonverbal gestures for communicating the need to refocus.

- Avoid pop quizzes and unexpected assessments.

- Eliminate "whole class" punishments; address problem behaviors one-on-one.

- Consider alternatives to traditional class-wide behavior-management systems, such as daily color or number charts. Instead, use more one-on-one feedback approaches to reduce self-consciousness.

- Prepare parents for receiving less frequent (i.e., not daily) feedback, especially with young children. Weekly or even biweekly feedback allows more time for children to respond to interventions. Given that development is not linear, less frequent feedback also highlights the need to look at trends and patterns versus daily episodes.

Tips for Reducing Test Anxiety

Children whose anxiety includes perfectionism, overachievement, and preoccupation with their future are more likely to experience test anxiety. The following recommendations are designed to reduce the impact of test anxiety on children's performance. Keep in mind that children who have learning disorders are also more at risk and usually benefit from specialized accommodations.

- Avoid using a dramatic or negative tone when discussing tests. Instead, use empowering language and a positive tone: "We have a math test on Friday, and I know that everyone can become well prepared."

- Avoid discussing negative implications of poor test performance. Instead, highlight the use and benefits of effective study skills. For example, rather than saying "If you don't do well on this test, you won't be ready for the next grade," use "Remember to review your flashcards at home this week so you can do well on the test."

- Teach study and test-taking skills in the classroom and provide practice tests during class time.

- Consider collaborative pretests in which students work together to practice and learn from each other before taking their own exams.

Reducing Task Avoidance

It is commonplace to label children who procrastinate or avoid doing required tasks as "lazy." In actuality, these children are usually experiencing anxiety and overwhelm that takes the form of procrastination and task avoidance. Avoidance can also be fueled by lack of interest, boredom, or a perception that the task is not relevant to them. The following tips may assist you in helping the children in your family or classroom become less avoidant and more productive.

Note: Avoidant children are more likely to have significant problems with self-regulation, and some may meet the criteria for neurodevelopmental disorders such as ADHD or autism. In such cases, task avoidance is unlikely to improve significantly without disorder-specific treatment; it may be necessary to seek guidance from a mental health professional.

- Assign short increments of work to promote persistence.

- Allow for brief movement breaks, which can "reboot" the brain for better performance.

- Considering rewarding/reinforcing completed increments of work with playful exchanges such as riddles or brainteasers.

- Predictable routine is key to success—"same time, same place." Designate a specific and mutually agreed-upon location in the home, such as the dining room table, for task completion. If the household is typically too distracting, consider alternative environments, such as the local library.

- Parallel work (seeing others working near them) may promote productivity.

- Minimize distractions. However, some children may find continuous background noise (such as calm music or white noise) beneficial.

- Highlight effort and encourage problem-solving rather than immediately correcting errors.

Managing Homework Anxiety

Homework battles—and the associated anxiety for both kids and parents—are a dreaded issue for many households. Research shows that with the exception of reading, the benefits of traditional homework for young children (below sixth grade) is minimal at best (Hernandez, 2018). Unfortunately, systemic and societal pressures continue to burden young children and their parents with busywork that can interfere with a happier household.

Teachers can explore the possibility of creative, hands-on learning activities for young children instead of traditional homework such as worksheets. When homework is unavoidable, parents can use the following guidelines for easing the stress associated with required schoolwork at home.

- Collaboratively develop a homework schedule with options to increase your child's sense of control. For example, some children prefer to do homework as soon as possible after school, while others need more wind-down time beforehand. Children also differ as to whether they want to begin with more or less challenging work.

- Consider a "seesaw" approach in which your child alternates between two different subjects. This can help homework feel less monotonous, especially for children with short attention spans. (This approach can help adults too!)

- Avoid insisting that your child must do all of their homework before they are given free time. Instead, allow for brief breaks to help reduce persistence fatigue.

- Provide short-term incentives for completing more challenging homework.

- Avoid punishment or highly negative consequences for incomplete homework, as these measures only fuel frustration. Natural consequences from the school environment are more suitable and have greater impact.

- Remember that homework need not be perfect. Instead, homework should serve as practice or reinforcement and as feedback for teachers about the child's current knowledge. Although tempting, excessive help with homework is not beneficial in the long run.

- Consider the use of an older student mentor or professional tutor, especially if you and your child are frequently in conflict over homework.

Effective Consultation Between Educators and Clinicians

Given that children spend much of their lives in school, it's understandable that the school setting is a source of both anxiety contributors and potential solutions. Effective consultation between educators and mental health providers is vital for optimizing treatment outcomes with anxious children. Consider the following guidelines when consulting with school staff.

- Assess the relationship between the child's parents and teachers/school staff. Is it friendly and collaborative, or strained and adversarial? If the relationship is problematic, explore the communication history to determine the experiences that led to the parents' current feelings and perceptions.

- After obtaining consent from the parents, discuss their needs and preferences about what specific information you should share and with whom. Also, find out which school staff members are most likely to be open to consultation and which may not be so receptive.

- Encourage the parents to inform the school that you are happy to consult and be of service. I prefer that school staff contact my office to schedule a consultation time, as this usually signals their openness to collaboration.

- When collecting information, obtain each educator's perspective and concerns. Be sure to acknowledge and validate their concerns while appreciating the great effort they have already expended. I find that most teachers really need extra support and recognition, so be sure to commend them for their hard work and dedication.

- Attempt to obtain information about previous evaluations, interventions, and outcomes. What has and has not been useful so far?

- Display advocacy for all rather than appearing to align with the child, family, or school staff alone. Objectivity and careful choice of words go a long way.

- Once all the previous criteria are met, invite the school staff members to hear your impressions and offer guidance and recommendations in a collaborative manner.

CHAPTER 16

Change Can Be Challenging: Adjustment Disorder Interventions

Change may be the only constant in life, but an onslaught of changes can be extremely stressful for a kid, especially when they have no control over the life events causing their stress. While many kids adapt well with good parental support, others struggle considerably. Adjustment disorders tend to be viewed as less serious or impairing compared with other disorders, but research is clear that children who experience adjustment-related distress are significantly more at risk for psychological disorders in adulthood (Shevlin et al., 2019).

Recognizing these kids' need for professional help is critical, given both the short-term and long-term implications of untreated adjustment issues.

Although stressors such as the death of a pet, parental separation or divorce, and peer conflict are common, they can nevertheless be very impactful. Other stressors can be highly unexpected or tragic, which may lead to symptoms ranging from distress to anxiety to trauma. Children's reactions vary greatly based on a number of factors, including temperament, preexisting psychological conditions, and access to support and resources. These factors largely determine a child's degree of resilience and have implications for future well-being. While traumatization unfortunately occurs for some, trauma treatment is an area of specialization beyond the scope of this book. I will simply encourage you to keep in mind that some anxious children are also experiencing trauma and thus need additional resources.

This chapter provides intervention guidance and exercises designed to facilitate healthy coping and resilience in children who are experiencing life stressors. Common stressors are addressed, such as those related to death and loss, parents' marital conflict and divorce, blended family challenges, and peer harassment. Family involvement is critical for effectively treating adjustment disorders, as many childhood stressors stem from the decisions, emotional states, and behaviors of the adults in their lives.

How I Feel About the Changes in My Life

Changes happen in everybody's lives. We will like some of life's changes, feel unsure about some, and definitely not like others. When change causes a lot of stress, we can become very anxious. But over time and with practice, we can learn to expect change and face it head-on rather than fear it. Think about the recent changes in your life to figure out which ones you like, which ones you may be confused about, and which ones you find very stressful or difficult.

1. These are the changes that I really like:

   _____

   _____

   _____

   _____

   _____

2. The changes that I am unsure about or that confuse me are:

   _____

   _____

   _____

   _____

   _____

3. The most stressful or difficult changes for me are:

   _____

   _____

   _____

   _____

   _____

Asking for Help With Tough Changes

When life throws big changes at us, it's important to ask for help from other people we trust. Talking about our worries, fears, and disappointments with others can help us think more positively and feel more okay about the changes in our lives. We can also get ideas about what we can do to get used to these changes. We might even start looking forward to the good things that can happen! Answer the following questions to make asking for help a little bit easier.

1. Which adults in your family can help you deal with tough changes?

_____

_____

_____

_____

2. Who are other adults you trust that you can talk with about stressful changes in your life?

_____

_____

_____

_____

3. Which friends of yours can you talk to about these changes? Maybe some of them have experienced tough changes too.

_____

_____

_____

_____

Talking to My Child About Difficult Changes

Chances are that you and your family will experience a significant change at some point. Whether it's a change you welcome or one you dread, your child will follow your lead in accepting and adjusting to it. Helping your child prepare for change depends largely on your emotional tone, which is conveyed not only through your words but through your facial expression, body posture, tone of voice, and behavior. For example, if you tell your child that the change will be positive, but moments later your child sees you pacing in worry, your optimistic comments will have little impact.

Discussing upcoming changes with your kid can be daunting. It's often hard to know if you're sharing too much or too little. What do they need (and not need) to know? How do you answer unexpected questions? How do you prepare for strong emotional reactions? Below are some step-by-step guidelines for having conversations with your kid about upcoming, potentially challenging changes.

- Before disclosing any information about a significant upcoming change, such as a parental residential separation, be sure to speak with the other relevant party first and reach consensus on what will be shared with your child. If this isn't possible, employ an objective third party, such as your child's therapist.

- Select an appropriate time and place to speak with your child. Be mindful of the other stressors in their life—for example, do not choose the night before your child has a big test, game, or performance. You may wish to ask your child's therapist to help facilitate the discussion in session, or you might plan to speak with your child one-on-one at home. Make sure your child will have plenty of free time in a safe space following your conversation, so they can process their feelings and use their coping skills as needed.

- When you speak with your child, begin with an introductory statement like:

  "I have an upcoming change to tell you about. You might feel ____ or ____ about the change, and that's okay. This change will be hard at first, but we will all work together so that it's not so hard over time."

- Once you've disclosed the information, observe and accept your child's reaction. If they run to their room, give them space for a while. If they become tearful or angry, reflect and validate the feeling but do *not* immediately offer reassurance:

  "It's okay to feel ____. Lots of kids feel this way at first."

- If your child is minimally responsive, do *not* ask them what they think or feel. Instead, *invite* them to share:

  > "Kids often have lots of different thoughts and feelings about changes like this. You can talk about them with me when you are ready."

- Many children will begin asking a series of "why" or "what-if" questions. Avoid being pressured to answer. Instead, address these questions with statements that reassure your child that you are in control and that you care:

  > "It's understandable to have lots of questions or worries. All I know right now is ____. But I will answer your questions as I find out more and after I have time to think so that I can give you good answers. It's hard to not know everything that's going to happen, but I will let you know more as soon as I can."

- Trust your parental instincts about the type and degree of reassurance to provide. Some kids will need physical affection, while others will respond better to validation and verbal reassurance. Some may also need some immediate help with self-soothing, redirection, or both:

  > "I know this isn't easy to hear. This all seems overwhelming right now, but we will help you get through these changes. Is there anything we can do right now that might help you feel better?"

Supporting Children Dealing With Grief and Loss

Children's early experiences with loss often involve the death of a grandparent or a cherished pet, although some face the untimely death of a parent, friend, or classmate. The following paragraphs offer some reminders of how to support children at different developmental levels through the grieving process, as well as how to assist parents who may be grieving as well.

Developmental level is a significant influence on a child's grieving process. Very young children (under age 5) have a very limited understanding of death, making them likely to ask about the whereabouts of the deceased pet or person for several weeks or more. Encourage the parents to provide extra comfort and nurturance, as well as validation regarding how very hard it is when you miss someone, rather than trying to get the child to understand the permanence of death.

Children between 5 and 7 years are beginning to understand the permanence of death, but still display considerable confusion about it, coupled with very limited self-control. I prepare parents for the likelihood of behavioral and developmental regression, such as bedwetting and tantrums. Children this age will also require extra support in terms of one-on-one time and assistance with self-soothing. Expression through art and play can be very helpful for this age range.

Once children turn 8 years of age, they begin using logic, although they are still quite egocentric and limited in their ability to apply such logic due to continued challenges with emotional regulation.

Children ages 8 to 10 will be much more inquisitive about the nature of the loss, frequently asking numerous questions that can prove quite challenging for parents. Help parents address the questions they are unable to answer by teaching them to reflect, normalize, and validate the feelings associated with these questions. For example, "why" questions often represent the struggle to accept the loss and wishing they had the power to bring the loved one back. "Why" is also commonly used to reflect sadness.

Preteens (ages 11 to 12) are becoming more intellectually sophisticated and may ask very philosophical, existential questions about loss. Such questions can leave parents feeling unprepared and at a loss as to how to answer. I relieve some of the burden by reminding parents that none of us can definitively answer such big questions. However, we all find ways to cope over time, even without clear answers. Kids in this age range vary greatly, often based on their temperament, as to how much they wish to discuss the loss versus distract themselves from the pain. Allowing kids to express themselves in creative ways—journaling, drawing, music, and so forth—can promote healthy grieving. Preteens may also display regressive behavior or seek more reassurance and one-on-one time with trusted adults.

Adolescents have a clear understanding of death, but their hormone-flooded brains and limited impulse control can lead to highly emotional reactions. Teens are notorious for displacing their grief onto others. Prepare the parents for erratic behavior and angry episodes in which the parents and other adults are blamed for everything under the sun. Grieving teens need a balance of alone time, organic (rather than planned) one-on-one time with parents, and lots of time with friends. I gently remind parents that teens are still struggling with self-control, so the more they as parents can self-regulate, the better. Encourage parental self-care to promote patience and curb the possibility of excessive discipline. Lengthy social restrictions and indefinite privilege or device revocation only heightens resentment and complicates the grieving process.

Keep in mind that some grieving teens will withdraw from others and may isolate for periods of time. While it is important to respect teens' alone time, I usually suggest parents inform their teen to expect a "touch-base" from them approximately every hour. This can allow parents to stay connected, which is vital because some grieving teens are at risk for depression.

Finally, recognize the needs of grieving parents by encouraging them to find comfort in trusted family or friends, or to perhaps reach out for therapeutic services themselves. Remind them to create time for self-care and leisure activities. I like referring to the "airline philosophy" of putting on your own oxygen mask before assisting others—we can't help anyone if we are gasping for breath.

Creative Corner

Play and art are a child's work. They are also powerful tools for helping kids through challenging life changes, losses, or other stressors. Family, animal, and fantasy figures, puppets, art supplies, and so forth are essential for assisting children with emotional expression and processing. Game play therapy is especially helpful for addressing interpersonal or relational problems with peers and family. Consider play therapy training if it is not already a part of your therapeutic repertoire.

How Are My Relationship Issues Affecting My Child Emotionally?

Our adult relationships can become quite complicated, and they often affect our children more than we realize. We tend to underestimate young children's awareness of adult tensions and overestimate their ability to cope. Remember that children are sensitive receivers but limited interpreters. Reflect on your own relationship status and complete the sentences below to determine what your child may be thinking and feeling about the relationships between the adults in their life, and what you can do to promote your child's adjustment.

1. How would I describe my relationship with my spouse/partner/significant other? _____

   _____

   _____

   _____

2. How would I describe my relationship with my child's other parent (if this is a different person

   from the one I just described)? _____

   _____

   _____

   _____

3. What challenging family dynamics in my household could be stressful to my child? _____

   _____

   _____

   _____

   _____

   _____

4. How is my own emotional state affected by the relationship issues in my life? _____

_____

_____

_____

_____

5. Although my child may or may not fully grasp the details of the relationship issues in our family,

they could be thinking _____

_____

and may be feeling _____

_____.

6. What changes can I make in how I relate to my child that could reduce their possible anxiety or

distress? _____

_____

_____

_____

Managing Life in Two Different "Household Bubbles"

If your parents live in two different places, going back and forth between these homes can be really hard, especially if the rules in each home are very different. Here's an exercise that might help:

- Think of your two different households as their own bubbles, each with its own set of things you can and can't do, as well as things you like and don't like.

- In each of the bubble houses below, write three things that make that bubble different from the other bubble. Your therapist can help you if you get stuck.

- Then, on the next page, write down one thing you wish each parent would do that would make dealing with the different bubbles a little easier for you.

1. I wish _____

   would _____ to

   make it easier for me to deal with the two different bubbles.

2. And I wish _____

   would _____ to

   make it easier for me to manage my two different bubbles.

Mind Your Own Bubble: Accepting the Differences Between Your Child's Two Households

Successful co-parenting is no easy task, especially when post-divorce/separation conflict is occurring. Children adapt best when both households function in a similar manner regarding homework, bedtime, and so forth. However, such consistency is rarely reached when the parents disagree about these matters. When parents attempt to influence how the other parent runs their household, children feel the tension—and this tension often increases the child's anxiety even more than the stress associated with the differences or the separation itself.

Rather than insisting that the other parent change how they do things, consider "minding your own bubble." This exercise can help you find ways to support your child in managing the differences they experience between the two households, which will ultimately reduce your child's distress.

1. In each of the "bubble houses" below, write down three main concerns about how this household differs from the other.

2. Now identify three ways that you can support your child's ability to cope with the transition from one household to the other. Providing your child with 15 to 30 minutes of adjustment time upon entering your household, rather than immediately questioning or directing them, can also help with the transition.

_____

_____

_____

Equipping Kids to Handle Peer Harassment

Sadly, peer harassment is a stressor that many children will face, whether it be in school, around their neighborhood, or on the playground. Children are often instructed by well-intentioned adults to ignore their harassers, to "stand up to them" (without an explanation of how to do so), or to state that their "feelings are hurt" and to "please stop." None of these responses are effective; in fact, they often strengthen the harassment.

Instead, consider the following approach for equipping and empowering kids in the face of hostile peer encounters.

- First, discover the exact nature of the harassment. The more specific information you obtain, the more effective your intervention. For example, what phrases are being used? Where does the behavior occur? How many kids are taking part in the harassment? What is the nature of your client's relationship with the kids they are finding problematic? How have they responded to the harassment thus far, and what has been the outcome?

- Next, determine if any adults are aware of the occurrences. If so, have these adults advised or assisted in any way? If adult intervention has occurred, did it help, have no effect, or worsen the situation? When adults have not been informed, collaborate with the child to obtain consent for informing parents and obtaining their assistance.

- Both kids and adults differ widely in their use of the term "bullying," which specifically involves a significant and ongoing power differential. While virtually all bullying includes harassment, not all harassment involves bullying. While both problems require attention, bullying requires a more detailed and comprehensive approach. When bullying is the issue, provide parents guidance about how to best inform the school (or the appropriate adults in the setting where the bullying is occurring). With harassment, attempt intervention with the parents and child before potentially involving other authority figures.

- Over the years, I've found effectively dealing with peer harassment to be quite a challenge. We all know what *doesn't* work, but helping children navigate the cruel behavior of their peers is far from easy. However, I think I've stumbled upon an essential ingredient: indifference. This means helping kids understand that while it's generally healthy to express your true thoughts and feelings to others, doing so with someone who is treating you poorly is *not* a good idea. I tell my clients how important it is to show mean kids that you *just don't care what they say.*

Essentially, my goal is for children to respond to unkind words in a way that helps them feel empowered rather than victimized. But indifference alone isn't quite enough, which is why I teach kids to "throw shade in an okay way." Shade can take the form of a little dismissive sarcasm, such as "Oh, were you talking just now? I didn't notice you were there." Children with a good sense of humor can be encouraged to incorporate their humor with your help. If the harasser responds, the next statement should be one of disengagement: "Well, whatever—I'm outta here." The final step is encouraging the child to immediately find one or more friends as a safe haven.

- Role play with your client, initially with them as the harasser, so you can get a genuine sense of how the child perceives the harassment. While role-playing as your client, use a variety of indifferent statements spoken in an empowered tone: "Oh, you like saying mean things. Got it. See ya later!" or "Ummm, I really don't listen to people who say stuff like that. Bye." Explore a variety of both indifference and disengagement phrases with kids until they identify with a few, or help them come up with their own. Assist them in making sure they choose statements that won't get them in trouble and encourage them to use an assertive tone, but not to yell or use inappropriate language, as the goal is to be empowered and indifferent but not unkind or hostile. Essentially, you're teaching them to stand up for themselves in a practical manner that establishes boundaries.

- After obtaining the child's consent, inform their parents about this approach. The parents can help by further strengthening the child's ability to effectively respond to unkind peers. Consulting with the child's school can also be helpful, especially to ensure that teachers and other staff understand the efforts to increase the child's assertiveness.

TREATMENT HIGHLIGHTS

- Adjustment disorder intervention is critical for promoting better coping in both childhood and adulthood.

- Provide kids with opportunities for discussing life changes that they like, dislike, or feel confused or uncertain about.

- After preparing parents with response guidance, encourage children to seek support with difficult changes.

- Consider a child's developmental level when addressing grief and loss, and help parents recognize their child's developmental strengths and limitations.

- Remind parents that their personal relationships and emotional well-being can hinder or promote their child's adjustment.

- Use the "bubble technique" to assist both children and parents with conflictual two-household situations.

- Teach kids how to display indifference and "throw shade in an okay way" in response to peer harassment.

CHAPTER 17

Measuring Progress: Rethinking Our Expectations and Goals

Throughout this book, many methods, strategies, and techniques have been shared to help children and their parents better understand, identify, and manage anxiety with the goal of improving children's quality of life. But how do we really know if our therapeutic efforts are having a positive impact? And when is the appropriate time for assessing treatment progress?

While there is no definitive time period for determining a child's or their parents' response to treatment, consider the following:

- Has good rapport been established with both the child and their parents? Lack of rapport reduces the necessary collaboration between you and the family.

- Have therapy sessions been consistent for at least two to three months? This includes sessions for the child, the parents, and any family work.

- Have you determined the most critical areas for intervention and conducted treatment accordingly? For example, if parent-child communication continues to be problematic, have adequate parent or family sessions been held?

- Have you consulted with other relevant adults in the child's family and school (or any other significant environment)?

- Have you considered any referrals for additional evaluation or services that could be beneficial (e.g., neurological, educational, or speech/language)?

Once you have determined and addressed those areas in need of further attention and you feel relatively confident about the treatment, you're in a good position to assess the degree of progress that has occurred. Now is the time to collaborate in a discussion of treatment progress with the parents and with the child in an age-appropriate manner. When progress has been minimal despite consistent treatment—especially when anxiety plays a strong hereditary role in the family—conversations about additional treatment approaches, such as medication, may be needed.

Following are several simple but effective methods for assessing treatment progress. Some are best suited for your own use, while others can be completed by your child clients and their parents.

Self-Reflection as a Parent of an Anxiety-Prone Child

By now, you have certainly learned quite a lot about parenting an anxiety-prone child. Answer the following questions to reflect on the progress you've made in helping your child have a healthier, less anxiety-ridden life.

1. How have I changed the way I communicate and relate with my child?

   _____

   _____

   _____

2. What change in myself do I see as most effective in helping me parent my distressed child?

   _____

   _____

   _____

3. What have I learned about things that contribute to my child's anxiety?

   _____

   _____

   _____

4. What have I learned that helps soothe and empower my child?

   _____

   _____

   _____

5. What can I identify as an area for my growth as a parent of an anxiety-prone child?

   _____

   _____

What Have I Learned About Anxiety and What Do I Do Differently?

Wow! You have learned a ton about anxiety and how to better manage it. Answer the following questions to see just how much progress you have made!

1. What does anxiety really mean? What is it, and what isn't it?

   _____

   _____

   _____

   _____

   _____

2. How do I now calm myself when I'm anxious?

   _____

   _____

   _____

   _____

   _____

3. What kinds of things do I now say to myself when I am anxious?

   _____

   _____

   _____

   _____

   _____

4. What behaviors usually help me feel less anxious?

_____

_____

_____

_____

5. When and how do I ask others for help with anxiety?

_____

_____

_____

_____

6. What is something that I need to practice more to help me when I'm anxious?

_____

_____

_____

_____

Using the BASE Method to Assess My Child's Progress

As a parent, you likely have a good sense of how your child is doing. However, you may be wondering what information will be most helpful to provide to your child's mental health provider to assess your child's progress. Here is a simple method for determining how your child is functioning in four key areas: behavior, academics, social relations, and emotional functioning (BASE). For each area, think about how your child has been doing over the past two to four weeks.

- **B = Behavior**
  How would I describe my child's overall behavior? Cooperative? Reasonable? Intense? Aggressive?

- **A = Academics**
  How is my child doing with schoolwork and learning? Is my child concerned with their academic performance, and if so, moderately or excessively?

- **S = Social Relations**
  How would I describe my child's social interactions and relationships with peers and adults? Is my child friendly and outgoing or timid and withdrawn?

- **E = Emotional Functioning**
  How would I describe my child's overall disposition? Are they generally happy and able to recover from distress with support, or are they typically irritable and difficult to soothe or comfort?

When one or more areas are predominantly problematic over a two-to-four-week period, this may signal a need for a change in treatment, environment, intervention, or medication. Be sure to discuss any areas of concern with your child's therapist.

FIDA: A Simple Strategy for Evaluating Response to Treatment

The BASE method described in the previous parent handout (p. 181) may also be useful in determining areas of progress and for future intervention. However, a more clinical approach that focuses on evaluating a child's anxiety symptoms can also be effective in assessing the child's current level of distress and overall functioning. This strategy is called the FIDA approach. Each letter of this acronym refers to a child's current anxiety manifestations relative to earlier in their treatment.

- **F = Frequency**

  Has the child's anxiety expression or experience become more or less frequent?

- **I = Intensity**

  When anxiety or distress does occur, is the experience seen as more or less intense? (Consider this from the child's perspective, the parents', and your own.)

- **D = Duration**

  When anxiety episodes occur, are they longer or shorter in duration than before?

- **A = Atypical Aspects**

  As a provider, would you consider the child's level of anxiety as highly, moderately, or minimally typical (i.e., to be expected) given current or recent psychosocial stressors and developmental factors?

  For example, if a child experienced a recent death in the family, their anxiety would typically be high. However, if a child's anxiety is quite frequent, intense, and of long duration in the absence of any identifiable factors, then this would be highly atypical. The more atypical the child's anxiety seems to be, the more likely it is that neurobiological/physiological factors are underpinning it. Atypical anxiety expressions are more common in families that have a considerable history of anxiety in more than one generation.

Rethinking and Modifying Our Expectations and Goals

This book wouldn't be complete without considering some of the major societal forces kids face. We all want kids to achieve reasonable educational goals, acquire necessary technological skills, and of course, live in a safe world. However, many adults who participate in the lives of children are hyperfocused on early academic achievement and preoccupied with the notion of safety to a degree that children are discouraged from taking healthy risks necessary for emerging into adulthood. Furthermore, we tend to send mixed messages about technology by expecting kids to be tech-savvy, but not tech-consumed.

Researchers such as Jean Twenge (2017) have found that despite our best intentions, many children are growing up anxious and ill-prepared for the responsibilities of adulthood. With this in mind, I offer the following recommendations for mental health providers, parents, teachers, and other adults who are involved in kids' lives. These suggestions will help us rethink and modify traditional expectations and goals so that children not only grow up less anxious, but with a healthier mindset that promotes a happier, calmer, and more fulfilling adulthood.

Encouraging Achievement Versus Overachievement

- Use more developmentally minded curriculum.

- Focus on process and effort over outcome.

- Replace "You're so smart" with "You've worked so hard, and it shows!"

- Replace "Maybe this isn't your thing" with "This is hard for lots of kids, and you'll improve with practice."

- Replace "Do your best" with "Do what you can."

- Integrate more collaborative learning approaches.

- Avoid both the "rat race" and "everybody gets a trophy" philosophies.

- Promote self-improvement rather than competition with peers.

- Increase time for free play and leisure (for both kids and adults).

Balancing Safety With Healthy Risk-Taking

- Promote awareness of surroundings and teach how to assess trustworthiness in others.

- Avoid terms such as "stranger danger"; instead, say, "Don't do what strangers tell you to do."

- Avoid helicopter parenting to promote self-reliance.

- Promote and model healthy risk-taking.

- Avoid catastrophizing; instead, develop touch-base communication tactics.

- Speak credibly and calmly, and recognize your emotional impact on youth.

- Gradually shift from protection to empowerment.

- Remember that kids self-regulate better around well-regulated adults.

Promoting Healthier Technology Usage

- Limit early childhood exposure to technology; hands-on activities are vital.

- Recognize device usage as an escape from distress and teach self-soothing skills.

- Provide education about social media and technology early, using adults as models.

- Consider ways to encourage a social media curriculum at school and home.

- For preteens and younger children, advise social media be used only through parents' accounts and with supervision.

- Devices for preteens and younger kids should be borrowed from the parents versus owned by the kids.

- Use technology schedules, including "no-tech times."

- Connect more in real time as a family.

TREATMENT HIGHLIGHTS

- Assess treatment progress by considering the quality of rapport (with the parents and child), treatment consistency, and whether the most critical areas for intervention have been targeted.

- Explore consultation with other significant adults in the child's life beyond the immediate family.

- Teach parents the BASE method for tracing their child's behavioral, academic, social, and emotional progress.

- Use the FIDA strategy to evaluate response to treatment by considering the frequency, intensity, duration, and possible atypical aspects of a child's symptoms.

- Consider referrals for additional evaluation or medication consultation.

- Keep in mind the societal forces kids face, and help parents set reasonable goals and expectations for their children.

Closing Thoughts

If you've read through this book, then you and I definitely have something in common: We are both passionate about the emotional well-being of children and adolescents. While I certainly enjoy providing therapy to adults, I find my work with young people to be especially inspiring. When I first began my clinical career, I didn't expect to be so moved by observing how children and their families not only cope but thrive in a world that seems to become more anxiety-inducing over time. I am truly grateful for being in the unique position of serving as a supportive guide for the dedicated, loving, courageous families that enter my office. I bet you feel the same way. My intention in writing this book was to provide you with greater clarity and a robust set of tools for your practice. I wish you continued strength as you strive to empower anxious children and their parents.

References

For your convenience, purchasers can download and print the worksheets from this book from **www.pesi.com/steveobrien**

Afzal, U. (2018). *Mindfulness for children: Help your child to be calm and content from breakfast till bedtime.* Kyle Books.

Al Salman, Z. H., Al Debel, F. A., Al Zakaria, F. M., Shafey, M. M., & Darwish, M. A. (2020). Anxiety and depression and their relation to the use of electronic devices among secondary school students in Al-Khobar, Saudi Arabia, 2018–2019. *Journal of Family & Community Medicine, 27*(1), 53–61. https://doi.org/10.4103/jfcm.JFCM_140_19

Centers for Disease Control and Prevention. (2022, September 7). *Sleep and sleep disorders.* https://sleepeducation.org/cdc-americans-sleep-deprived/

Delahooke, M. (2017). *Social and emotional development in early intervention: A skills guide for working with children.* PESI Publishing & Media.

Delahooke, M. (2019). *Beyond behaviors: Using brain science and compassion to understand and solve children's behavioral challenges.* PESI Publishing and Media.

Fields, A., Harmon, C., Lee, Z., Louie, J. Y., & Tottenham, N. (2021). Parent's anxiety links household stress and young children's behavioral dysregulation. *Developmental Psychobiology, 63*(4), 16–30. https://doi.org/10.1002/dev.22013

Gerlach, A. L., & Gloster, A. T. (2020). *Generalized anxiety disorder and worrying: A comprehensive handbook for clinicians and researchers.* Wiley Blackwell.

Halloran, J. (2018). *Coping skills for kids workbook: Over 75 coping strategies to help kids deal with stress, anxiety and anger.* PESI Publishing & Media.

Hernandez, S. (2018, December 17). Elementary schools embrace reading at home as they downplay homework assignments. *Green Bay Press-Gazette.* https://www.greenbaypressgazette.com/story/news/education/2018/12/17/elementary-schools-trading-homework-reading/1905818002/

Hiller, R. M., Apetroaia, A., Clarke, K., Hughes, Z., Orchard, F., Parkinson, M., & Creswell, C. (2016). The effect of targeting tolerance of children's negative emotions among anxious parents of children with anxiety disorders: A pilot randomised controlled trial. *Journal of Anxiety Disorders, 42,* 52–59. https://doi.org/10.1016/j.janxdis.2016.05.009

Hofmann, S. G., & DiBartolo, P. M. (2014). *Social anxiety: Clinical, developmental, and social perspectives* (3rd ed.). Academic Press.

Jiang, L. C., Yang, I. M., & Wang, C. (2017). Self-disclosure to parents in emerging adulthood: Examining the roles of perceived parental responsiveness and separation–individuation. *Journal of Social and Personal Relationships, 34*(4), 425–445. https://doi.org/10.1177/0265407516640603

Kaduson, H. G., & Schaefer, C. E. (2021). *Play therapy with children: Modalities for change.* American Psychological Association. https://doi.org/10.1037/0000217-000

Lebrun-Harris, L. A., Ghandour, R. M., Kogan, M. D., & Warren, M. D. (2022). Five-year trends in US children's health and well-being, 2016–2020. *JAMA Pediatrics, 176*(7), Article e220056. https://doi.org/10.1001/jamapediatrics.2022.0056

Lewin, A. B., & Storch, E. A. (Eds.). (2017). *Understanding OCD: A guide for parents and professionals.* Jessica Kingsley Publishers.

McCrindle, M., & Fell, A. (with Buckerfield, S.). (2021). *Generation Alpha: Understanding our children and helping them thrive.* Headline Publishing Group.

Meersand, P., & Gilmore, K. J. (2018). *Play therapy: A psychodynamic primer for the treatment of young children.* American Psychiatric Association Publishing.

Nagy, S. (2017). The impact of country of origin in mobile phone choice of Generation Y and Z. *Journal of Management and Training for Industries, 4*(2), 16–29. https://doi.org/10.12792/JMTI.4.2.16

Otto, M. W., & Smits, J. A. J. (2011). *Exercise for mood and anxiety: Proven strategies for overcoming depression and enhancing well-being.* Oxford University Press.

Peckmann, C., Kannen, K., Pensel, M. C., Lux, S., Philipsen, A., & Braun, N. (2022). Virtual reality induces symptoms of depersonalization and derealization: A longitudinal randomized control trial. *Computers in Human Behavior, 131,* Article 107233. https://doi.org/10.1016/j.chb.2022.107233

Pendry, P., & Adam, E. K. (2007). Associations between parents' marital functioning, maternal parenting quality, maternal emotion and child cortisol levels. *International Journal of Behavioral Development, 31*(3), 218–231. https://doi.org/10.1177/0165025407074634

Saneei, P., Hajishafiee, M., Hassanzadeh Keshteli, A., Afshar, H., Esmaillzadeh, A., & Adibi, P. (2016). Adherence to alternative healthy eating index in relation to depression and anxiety in Iranian adults. *British Journal of Nutrition, 116*(2), 335–342. https://doi.org/10.1017/S0007114516001926

Schwartz, B. (2005). *The paradox of choice* [Video]. TEDGlobal 2005. https://www.ted.com/talks/barry_schwartz_the_paradox_of_choice?language=en

Schwarzfischer, P., Gruszfeld, D., Stolarczyk, A., Ferre, N., Escribano, J., Rousseaux, D., Moretti, M., Mariani, B., Verduci, E., Koletzko, B., & Grote, V. (2019). Physical activity and sedentary behavior from 6 to 11 years. *Pediatrics, 143*(1), Article e20180994. https://doi.org/10.1542/peds.2018-0994

Shapiro, S., & Weisbaum, E. (2020). History of mindfulness and psychology. *Oxford Research Encyclopedias.* http//doi.org/10.1093/acrefore/9780190236557.013.678

Shevlin, M., Hyland, P., Ben-Ezra, M., Karatzias, T., Cloitre, M., Vallières, F., Bachem, R., & Maercker, A. (2019). Measuring ICD-11 adjustment disorder: The development and initial validation of the international adjustment disorder questionnaire. *Acta Psychiatrica Scandinavica, 141*(3), 265–274. https://doi.org/10.1111/acps.13126

Sparks, D. (2007). *Leading for results: Transforming teaching, learning, and relationships in schools* (2nd ed.). Corwin Press.

Steinberg, L. (2015). *Age of opportunity: Lessons from the new science of adolescence.* Mariner Books.

Suler, J. (2006). The online disinhibition effect. *International Journal of Applied Psychoanalytic Studies, 2*(2), 184–188. https://doi.org/10.1002/aps.42

Taveras, E. M., Rifas-Shiman, S. L., Bub, K. L., Gillman, M. W., & Oken, E. (2017). Prospective study of insufficient sleep and neurobehavioral functioning among school-age children. *Academic Pediatrics, 17*(6), 625–632. https://doi.org/10.1016/j.acap.2017.02.001

Thomas, A., & Chess, S. (1977). *Temperament and development.* Brunner/Mazel Publishing.

Trigueros, R., Navarro, N., Mercader, I., Aguilar-Parra, J. M., Lopez-Liria, R., & Rocamora-Pérez, P. (2022). Self-stigma, mental health and healthy habits in parent of children with severe mental disorder. *Psychology Research and Behavior Management, 15*, 227–235. https://doi.org/10.2147/PRBM.S342780

Twenge, J. M. (2017). *iGen: Why today's super-connected kids are growing up less rebellious, more tolerant, less happy—and completely unprepared for adulthood (and what this means for the rest of us).* Atria Books.

Twenge, J. M. (2020). Why increases in adolescent depression may be linked to the technological environment. *Current Opinion in Psychology, 32*, 89–94. https://doi.org/10.1016/j.copsyc.2019.06.036

Yang, F. N., Xie, W., & Wang, Z. (2022). Effects of sleep duration on neurocognitive development in early adolescents in the USA: A propensity score matched, longitudinal observational study. *The Lancet Child & Adolescent Health, 6*(10), 705–712. https://doi.org/10.1016/S2352-4642(22)00188-2

Recommended Readings

Afzal, U. (2018). *Mindfulness for children: Help your child to be calm and content from breakfast till bedtime.* Kyle Books.

Alter, A. (2017). *Irresistible: The rise of addictive technology and the business of keeping us hooked.* Penguin Press.

Delahooke, M. (2017). *Social and emotional development: A skills guide for working with children.* PESI Publishing & Media.

Dorn, A. (2021). *Calm and peaceful mindful me.* PESI Publishing & Media.

Elmore, T. (with McPeak, A.). (2019). *Generation Z unfiltered: Facing nine hidden challenges of the most anxious population.* Poet Gardener Publishing.

Hurley, K. (2022). *The stress-buster workbook for kids: 75 evidence-based strategies to help kids regulate their emotions, build coping skills, and tap into positive thinking.* PESI Publishing.

Katz, R. Ogilvie, S., Shaw, J., & Woodhead, L. (2021). *Gen Z, explained: The art of living in a digital age.* The University of Chicago Press.

Lewin, A. B., & Storch, E. A. (Eds.). (2017). *Understanding OCD: A guide for parents and professionals.* Jessica Kingsley Publishers.

McCrindle, M., & Fell, A. (with Buckerfield, S.). (2021). *Generation Alpha: Understanding our children and helping them thrive.* Headline Publishing Group.

Twenge, J. M. (2017). *iGen: Why today's super-connected kids are growing up less rebellious, more tolerant, less happy—and completely unprepared for adulthood (and what this means for the rest of us).* Atria Books.

Washington, V. (2021). *Changing the game for Generation Alpha: Teaching and raising young children in the 21st century.* Redleaf Press.

Willard, C. (2021). *Mindfulness for teen anxiety: A workbook for overcoming anxiety at home, at school, and everywhere else* (2nd ed.). Instant Help Books.

Wu, J. (2023). *Hello sleep: The science and art of overcoming insomnia without medications.* St. Martin's Essentials.

About the Author

Steve O'Brien, PsyD, is a clinical psychologist with over 30 years of experience treating children, adolescents, and families in his Tampa Bay, Florida, practice. His specialty areas include treatment for childhood anxiety and depression, ADHD, autism spectrum disorders, and divorced/blended family adjustment. Dr. O'Brien has worked in a variety of settings, including community mental health centers, psychiatric hospitals, and medical clinics. He utilizes an integrative model that tailors treatment to the developmental level of both children and parents.

Dr. O'Brien earned his PsyD at Nova Southeastern University and received specialized training in applied developmental psychology. He is a national consultant and well-received speaker for PESI, training professionals in child and adolescent mental health treatment and complex family issues.

Dr. O'Brien has over 20 years of teaching experience at the graduate and undergraduate level. He served as an associate professor at the Florida School of Professional Psychology (now National Louis University) from 2000 to 2016, where he developed a unique course in Parent Consultation. In 2015, Dr. O'Brien developed Life@Home by Psychtouch.com, a first-of-its-kind clinical tool and app for obtaining a child's perception of their family life. Dr. O'Brien also serves as a media consultant for Spectrum Bay News 9, Tampa Bay's 24-hour news source.

Acknowledgments

Thank you to my family and friends for their enthusiasm and support during this project. I would also like to acknowledge the following people for their considerable contributions: My clients for their courage, candor, and commitment to the therapeutic process. The outstanding Kim Kirchoffer, whose belief in this book empowered me whenever I harbored doubt. The team at PESI, especially Meg, Kate, Chelsea, and Gretchen, for entrusting and guiding me with this project. And my mentor, Dr. Ruth Peters, for providing wisdom, guidance, and unexpected opportunities.